Personal Best

A1 Beginner

Student's Book and Workbook combined edition — B

Series Editor
Jim Scrivener

Student's Book Author
Graham Fruen

Workbook Author
Daniel Barber

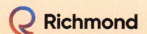

STUDENT'S BOOK CONTENTS

		LANGUAGE			SKILLS	
		GRAMMAR	PRONUNCIATION	VOCABULARY		
6	**Places**	• *there is/are* • prepositions of place	• linking consonants and vowels • sentence stress	• places in a town • parts of the body • rooms and furniture	**READING** • an article about art in public spaces • reading in detail • giving opinions	**SPEAKING** • checking information • asking for and giving directions **PERSONAL BEST** • a conversation asking for and giving directions
6A	City or town? p50					
6B	City art p52					
6C	An unusual home p54					
6D	Is there a post office near here? p56					
5 and **6**	**REVIEW and PRACTICE** p58					
7	**All in the past**	• simple past: *be* • simple past: regular verbs	• *was/were* • *-ed* endings	• celebrities • months and ordinals • time expressions	**LISTENING** • a video about Shakespeare and the theater • listening for dates • linking consonants and vowels	**WRITING** • writing informal e-mails • sequencers **PERSONAL BEST** • an e-mail about an interesting weekend
7A	When they were young p60					
7B	I was there in July p62					
7C	Famous decades p64					
7D	A weekend away p66					
8	**Travel**	• simple past: irregular verbs • *there was/were*	• irregular simple past verbs • sentence stress	• travel verbs • weather and seasons • nature	**READING** • posts about an unusual trip on a travel website • understanding the main idea • modifiers	**SPEAKING** • starting and ending a phone call at work • buying a ticket **PERSONAL BEST** • a phone call buying a ticket
8A	Incredible trips p68					
8B	Crazy weather! p70					
8C	Then and now p72					
8D	A trip to Canada p74					
7 and **8**	**REVIEW and PRACTICE** p76					
9	**Shopping**	• present continuous • *how often* + frequency expressions	• *-ing* endings • sentence stress	• clothes • feelings • shopping	**LISTENING** • a video about how our clothes affect how we feel • identifying key points • filler words	**WRITING** • describing a photo • describing position **PERSONAL BEST** • an e-mail describing a photo
9A	Street style p78					
9B	How do you feel? p80					
9C	Love it or hate it? p82					
9D	Garage sale p84					
10	**Time out**	• present continuous for future plans • question review	• sentence stress • intonation in questions	• free-time activities • types of music and movies • sports and games	**READING** • a listings page from an entertainment website • scanning for information • the imperative	**SPEAKING** • showing interest • asking about a tourist attraction **PERSONAL BEST** • a conversation about a tourist attraction
10A	What are you doing on the weekend? p86					
10B	What's on? p88					
10C	Royal hobbies p90					
10D	Where are we going now? p92					
9 and **10**	**REVIEW and PRACTICE** p94					

Grammar practice p101   **Vocabulary practice** p120   **Communication practice** p138   **Irregular verbs** p151

Language App, unit-by-unit grammar and vocabulary games

WORKBOOK CONTENTS

		LANGUAGE			SKILLS	
		GRAMMAR	PRONUNCIATION	VOCABULARY		
6 Places		• *there is/are* • prepositions of place	• linking consonants and vowels • sentence stress	• places in a town • parts of the body • rooms and furniture	READING • reading in detail	SPEAKING • asking for and giving directions
6A	p34					
6B	p35					
6C	p36					
6D	p37					
6 — REVIEW and PRACTICE	p38					
7 All in the past		• simple past: *be* • simple past: regular verbs	• *was/were* • *-ed* endings	• celebrities • months and ordinals • time expressions	LISTENING • listening for dates	WRITING • writing informal e-mails
7A	p40					
7B	p41					
7C	p42					
7D	p43					
7 — REVIEW and PRACTICE	p44					
8 Travel		• simple past: irregular verbs • *there was/were*	• irregular simple past verbs • sentence stress	• travel verbs • weather and seasons • nature	READING • understanding the main idea	SPEAKING • buying a ticket
8A	p46					
8B	p47					
8C	p48					
8D	p49					
8 — REVIEW and PRACTICE	p50					
9 Shopping		• present continuous • *how often* + frequency expressions	• *-ing* endings • sentence stress	• clothes • feelings • shopping	LISTENING • identifying key points	WRITING • describing a photo
9A	p52					
9B	p53					
9C	p54					
9D	p55					
9 — REVIEW and PRACTICE	p56					
10 Time out		• present continuous for future plans • question review	• sentence stress • intonation in questions	• free-time activities • types of music and movies • sports and games	READING • scanning for information	SPEAKING • asking about a tourist attraction
10A	p58					
10B	p59					
10C	p60					
10D	p61					
10 — REVIEW and PRACTICE	p62					

Writing practice **p67**

UNIT 6 Places

LANGUAGE — there is/are ■ places in town

6A City or town?

1 Match the words in the box with places 1–6.

bank   bus stop   restaurant
hotel   grocery store   post office

1 _____   3 _____   5 _____
2 _____   4 _____   6 _____

Go to Vocabulary practice: places in town, page 120

2 A Look at the pictures of Whycocomagh in Canada. Is it a city or a town?

B Read the text and check (✓) the things Whycocomagh has.

1 shopping mall ☐   3 movie theater ☐   5 school ☐
2 grocery store ☐   4 club ☐   6 restaurants ☐

An unusual job offer

Whycocomagh is a small town on the beautiful island of Cape Breton in Canada, but the local grocery store has a problem. It needs three new salesclerks, and people don't want to come to live in Whycocomagh because it's very quiet and far from any big cities.

So the owners of the Farmer's Daughter store put an unusual job posting on Facebook. It says, *"We can't give you big money, but we can give you an awesome life"* … and they offer over 2,000 acres of free land!

Thousands of people from around the world are interested and want to work in the town, so now the grocery store has some new salesclerks. But what's the town really like? We talk to Kelly Jenkins, a teacher at the local school.

Tell us about Whycocomagh, Kelly.
It's small, but it's beautiful. There's a school, a post office, and the local grocery store, of course! There are also some hotels and restaurants for tourists.

Is there a shopping mall or a movie theater?
No, there's not! There aren't any big stores and there's no movie theater or clubs. But there are some wonderful people here. Everyone is very friendly.

Are there any problems?
Yes, there are … but life's boring without any problems!

3 Complete the sentences with the words in the box. Check your answers in the text.

's no   's   aren't   are (x2)   is

1 There _____ a school.
2 _____ there a shopping mall?
3 There _____ any big stores.
4 There _____ movie theater.
5 There _____ some wonderful people.
6 _____ there any problems?

50

there is/are ■ places in a town **LANGUAGE 6A**

4 Look at the sentences in exercise 3 again and choose the correct options to complete the rules. Then read the Grammar box.
1 We use *there's* and *there's no* with **singular / plural** nouns.
2 We use *there are* and *there are no* with **singular / plural** nouns.
3 We use **some / any** with plural nouns in affirmative sentences.
4 We use **some / any** with plural nouns in negative sentences and questions.

Grammar *there is/are*

Affirmative:
There's a movie theater.
There are some stores.

Negative:
There's no museum.
There aren't any cafés. /
There are no cafés.

Questions:
Is there a park?
Are there any hotels?

Short answers:
Yes, there is.   No, there isn't.
Yes, there are. No, there aren't.

Go to Grammar practice: *there is/are*, page 101

5 In pairs, say if you want to live in Whycocomagh. Explain your answers.
I don't want to live in Wycocomagh because there ...

6 ▶ 6.3 Complete the text with the correct form of *there is/are*. Listen and check

This is the beautiful city of Lavasa in India. ¹_____ some nice apartments near the river. ²_____ a post office, a police station, and ³_____ also some great restaurants and cafés. ⁴_____ no train station, but if you need to travel by train, you can take a taxi to Pune, which is 60 kilometers away. However, ⁵_____ something strange about Lavasa … nobody lives here! ⁶_____ people in the apartments. On the weekend, ⁷_____ some tourists in the restaurants and hotels, but they're on vacation.

7 A ▶ 6.4 **Pronunciation: linking consonants and vowels** Listen and repeat the sentences from exercise 6. Pay attention to how the sounds link together.
1 There's‿a post‿office.
2 There's no‿train station.
3 There‿are no people.
4 There‿are some tourists.

B ▶ 6.5 Say the sentences linking the sounds together. Listen, check, and repeat.
1 There's‿a hospital.
2 Is there‿a bank?
3 There‿are some‿offices.
4 There‿are no‿museums.
5 There‿are some‿apartments.
6 Are there‿any old buildings?

Go to Communication practice: Student A page 138, Student B page 146

8 A ▶ 6.6 Listen to the conversation. Where does Erica live? Is she happy there?

B ▶ 6.6 Are the sentences about the area where Erica lives true (T) or false (F)? Listen again and check.
1 There's a big park. ____
2 There's a movie theater. ____
3 There are no stores. ____
4 There's a café in her street. ____
5 There's no bus stop near her house. ____
6 There are some good restaurants. ____

9 Ask and answer the questions in pairs.

> Where do you live?   Is it a city or town?   What's your area like?
> Is there a …?   Are there any …?

Personal Best Write about a city or town you know well.

6 SKILLS READING reading in detail ■ giving opinions ■ parts of the body

6B City art

1 A Look at the pictures of public art on page 53. Do you like them? Why/Why not?

B Read the text quickly. In which cities can you see the three pieces of art?

> **Skill** reading in detail
>
> We sometimes have to read part of a text in detail to understand it well.
> • Read the question and find the paragraph of the text that has the information you need.
> • Read the paragraph very carefully to answer the question.
> • We sometimes use different words and phrases to give the same information.

2 Read the Skill box. Choose the correct options to complete the sentences. <u>Underline</u> the phrase in the text that helped you answer the questions.

1 Carla and Mason have ____ .
 a jobs at the same hotel   b lots of cameras   c different opinions about *Eye*
2 Bruno Catalano ____ .
 a makes sculptures   b only has one arm   c is from Spain
3 Elodie and Christine ____ .
 a are friends of the artist   b live in Marseille   c are on vacation
4 Günther ____ the lifesaver fountain.
 a likes   b doesn't like   c doesn't give an opinion about
5 Helga works ____ .
 a in a school   b in a restaurant   c as a taxi driver

3 Match the words in the box with parts of the body 1–7 in the pictures on page 53.

head foot eye body leg hand arm

1 _____ 2 _____ 3 _____ 4 _____ 5 _____ 6 _____ 7 _____

Go to Vocabulary practice: parts of the body, page 121

4 Match the people with the opinions.

1 Carla   a "I don't think it means anything."
2 Mason   b "I like it."
3 Elodie and Christine c "I think this is really ugly."
4 Günther   d "In my opinion, that's what it means."
5 Helga   e "It's beautiful."

> **Text builder** giving opinions
>
> **Phrases:** *In my opinion, ...   In my view, ...*
> **Verbs:** *I think/don't think ...   I like/don't like ...*
> **Adjectives:** *It's beautiful/ugly/interesting/boring/strange*, etc.
>
> **Look!** We say: *I don't think it's ugly.*
> NOT ~~I think it isn't ugly.~~

5 Read the Text builder. In pairs, describe the sculptures in the pictures and give your opinions.

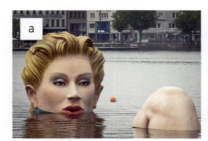
a

b

c

reading in detail ■ giving opinions ■ parts of the body   READING   SKILLS   6B

I love it ...
but what is it?

There's art everywhere in our towns, cities, and parks. Sometimes it's good, sometimes it's bad, but it's always interesting.

Eye
In the courtyard of a five-star hotel in Dallas, in Texas, there's a 32-foot-high eye, called *Eye*. "It's really interesting," says Carla, a receptionist at the hotel. "There are cameras everywhere today, watching us. In my opinion, that's what it means." Mason, a waiter from another hotel, doesn't agree. "I don't think it means anything," he says. "It's just an eye!"

Travelers
In Marseille, France, there's an amazing sculpture by the French artist Bruno Catalano. It's a man on a trip. He only has one arm and he has no body. "It's beautiful," say Elodie and her friend Christine, tourists from Paris. "Perhaps it means that when we leave a place, we leave a part of us behind."

Lifesaver fountain
This fountain in Duisburg in Germany is big and colorful. It has a person's legs, but a bird's head and feet. But what is it? And what do local people think? "I usually like modern art," says Günther, a taxi driver. "But I think this is really ugly." Helga, a teacher, disagrees. "I like it," she says. "I often have lunch in a restaurant on this street. When I see the fountain, I feel happy."

Personal Best Write about a piece of art you know and give your opinion of it.

53

6 LANGUAGE — prepositions of place ■ rooms and furniture

6C An unusual home

1 Match the furniture in the box with pictures a–f.

refrigerator   table   bed   sofa   closet   chair

 a
 b
 c
 d
 e
 f

Go to Vocabulary practice: rooms and furniture, page 122

2 In pairs, describe a room in your house. Can your partner guess the room?

A *There are four chairs in this room.*
A *No, it's my living room!*
B *Is it your kitchen?*

3 Look at the picture. Guess where Kirsten lives. Read the text and check.

Life on the water

For college students, a room in an apartment or a house can be very expensive, but not for 20-year-old Kirsten Müller. Kirsten is a student at a business school in Berlin … and she lives on a boat! It's small, but it's home.
Kirsten is on the sofa in the living room. There's a small table in front of her. "I study here every night," she says. "And I eat here too." The kitchen has an electric stove, and next to it, there's a small refrigerator. Kirsten cooks all her meals on the boat. "It's perfect for me, but I can't invite lots of friends for dinner!" The bedroom has a bed … and nothing else! All of Kirsten's clothes are in boxes under the bed because there's no closet. Between the bedroom and the kitchen, there's a modern bathroom with a shower and a toilet.
Kirsten loves her home. It's cheap, and the people on the other boats are friendly, but are there any problems? "I don't like getting up in the winter," she says. "It's very cold!"

4 Read the text again. Match the rooms in the box with the parts of the boat.

living room   bathroom   bedroom   kitchen

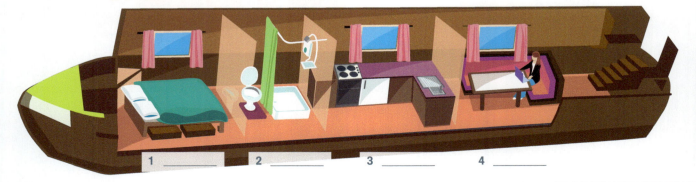

1 _____   2 _____   3 _____   4 _____

prepositions of place ■ rooms and furniture **LANGUAGE 6C**

5 Look at the diagram in exercise 4 again. Complete the sentences with the prepositions of place in the box. Check your answers in the text. Then read the Grammar box.

| under   between   in   on   next to   in front of |

1 Kirsten is _____ the sofa.
2 There's a small table _____ her.
3 The kitchen has an electric stove, and _____ it, there's a small refrigerator.
4 All of Kirsten's clothes are _____ boxes _____ the bed.
5 _____ the bedroom and the kitchen, there's a modern bathroom.

Grammar | **prepositions of place**

There's a table **next to** the sofa.
My cell phone is **in** my purse.
Your shoes are **under** the bed.
My keys are **on** the table.

My bedroom is **above** our living room.
Luca sits **between** Carlos and Emma.
Your car is **in front of** our house.
The cat is **behind** the sofa.

Go to Grammar practice: prepositions of place, page 101

6 ▶ 6.10 **Pronunciation:** sentence stress Listen and repeat the sentences. Pay attention to the underlined stressed words.

1 The camera is under my bed.
2 Your head is in front of the TV.
3 His shoes are next to the sofa.
4 The bathroom is behind the door.

7 A Complete the sentences with the correct prepositions of place.

1 The window is _____ the table.
2 Your keys are _____ the book.
3 The books are _____ the shelves.
4 There's a bed _____ the window and the chair.

B ▶ 6.11 In pairs, say the sentences with the correct stress. Listen, check, and repeat.

8 A ▶ 6.12 Look at the picture and listen to the description. Find six differences between the description and the picture.

B ▶ 6.12 Compare your answers in pairs. Listen again and check.

There's no clock on the table. There's a lamp on the table.

Go to Communication practice: Student A page 138, Student B page 146

9 A Think of a room in your house. Make notes about what furniture is in it and where it is.

B In pairs, describe your room. Your partner draws it. Then check your pictures.

10 Ask and answer the questions in pairs.
1 Do you live in a house or an apartment?
2 Which is your favorite room? Why?
3 Imagine your ideal bedroom/living room/kitchen. What's in it?

Personal Best Write about your "dream" home.

6 SKILLS SPEAKING checking information ■ asking for and giving directions

6D Is there a post office near here?

1 In pairs, discuss what you usually do when you're lost.
  a Ask someone in the street for directions.
  b Go into a store and ask for directions.
  c Look at a map.
  d Use a GPS app on your phone.
  e Walk around and hope you find the place.

2 ▶ 6.13 Watch or listen to the first part of *Learning Curve*. Choose the correct words to complete the sentences.
  1 Simon has *cereal and tea / eggs, toast, and coffee / eggs, toast, and tea* for breakfast.
  2 He never goes to work *by car / by bike / on the subway*.
  3 Kate always says *"the underground" / "the subway" / "the tube."*
  4 The man wants to find *a parking lot / a post office / the subway station*.

3 ▶ 6.13 Complete the conversation with phrases a–e. Watch or listen again, and check.

Man Excuse me. ¹_____	a It's on the left, near the car park.
Simon Yes, there is. ²_____ Go straight on. ³_____	b Thank you very much.
Man ⁴_____	c No problem.
Simon ⁵_____	d It's down the street.
	e Is there a post office around here?

Conversation builder — asking for and giving directions

Asking for directions:
Excuse me.
Is there a post office near here?
Is there a post office around here?
Where's the post office?

Giving directions:
Go straight on/ahead.
Go down this street.
Turn right/left at …
It's on the right/left/corner.
It's near/next to/across from …

4 A Read the Conversation builder. In pairs, look at the maps, and ask for and give directions to the orange places.

  A *Excuse me, where's the bank?*   B *Go straight ahead …*

B ▶ 6.14 Listen and check. Are your conversations similar?

checking information ■ asking for and giving directions **SPEAKING**   SKILLS **6D**

5 ▶ 6.15 Watch or listen to the second part of the show. Choose the correct options to answer the questions.

1 Where do the women want to go?
   a To the movie theater.
   b To the shopping center.
   c To the grocery store.

2 What's the problem at the studio?
   a There's no water.
   b There's no tea.
   c There's no electricity

6 ▶ 6.15 Watch or listen again. Complete the conversations with the phrases in the box.

a problem   show me   near here   did you say   repeat that   you mean

1 **Woman 1** Is there a shopping center ¹_____ ?
   Simon Yes, it's near the supermarket. Go down this street, turn right on Bethnal Green Road. Don't stop at Ebor Street. Go straight ahead.
   Woman 2 I'm sorry, ²_____ near the supermarket?

2 **Woman 1** Can you ³_____ on the map?
   Simon We're here. And there's the cinema. And there's the supermarket. The shopping center is next to the supermarket. See?
   Woman 2 Could you ⁴_____, please? More slowly.

3 **Kate** There's ⁵_____, so there's no water in the kitchen or the bathroom. But there's water under the receptionist's desk! Poor Marina.
   Simon I'm sorry, did you say there's a problem on the street? ⁶_____, a problem with the water?

🔧 **Skill**   checking information

If you don't understand what someone says, you can:
• ask him/her to repeat: *Could you repeat that, please?   Could you say that again?*
• ask him/her to speak more slowly: *Could you speak more slowly, please?*
• ask a question to check the information: *Did you say near the supermarket?   You mean, a problem with the water?*

7 A ▶ 6.16 Read the Skill box. Listen and match phrases a–d with conversations 1–4. Where are the people in the situations?
   a I'm sorry, did you say …? _____
   b I'm sorry, could you say that again, please? _____
   c I'm sorry, could you repeat that, please? _____
   d I'm sorry, could you speak more slowly, please? _____

B ▶ 6.16 Listen again and complete the information that the people repeat.
   1 Turn right at the _____ . Then turn _____ at the _____ .
   2 _____ . _____ @mail.com
   3 708 _____
   4 $ _____

Go to Communication practice: Student A page 139, Student B page 147

8 A PREPARE In pairs, think of four places in your town. Think about how to get to the places from where you are now.

   a train station or bus stop   a museum or tourist attraction
           a restaurant or café   a shopping mall or grocery store

B PRACTICE Ask for and give directions. Check the information if you don't understand something.

C PERSONAL BEST Swap partners and ask for and give directions to a new place. Are you more confident asking for directions in English?

Personal Best Write an e-mail to a friend with directions to your house from the bus or train station.

57

5 and 6 REVIEW and PRACTICE

Grammar

1 Choose the correct options to complete the sentences.

1 On Saturdays, I meet my friends _____ the shopping mall.
   a on   b under   c at
2 _____ shelves in the living room.
   a There are no
   b There
   c There's no
3 He can't _____ coffee. It's always horrible!
   a make   b to make   c makes
4 My friends live in the city. I meet _____ on the weekend.
   a they   b them   c us
5 There are _____ in the kitchen.
   a any cookies
   b some cookie
   c some cookies
6 Your sunglasses are _____ to my laptop.
   a on   b in front   c next
7 A Is there a hospital in your town?
   B Yes, _____ .
   a there's
   b there is
   c there are
8 _____ drive a truck?
   a Do you can
   b Can you
   c You can

2 Complete the conversations with the words in the box.

| are no   any   can   can't   her |
| 's no   it   next to   on   them |

1 A _____ you swim?
   B Yes, I can, but there _____ swimming pool in this town.
2 A Are there _____ restaurants near here?
   B Yes, there's an Italian restaurant _____ the grocery store on School Street.
3 A Where are my headphones? I want to use _____ .
   B They're _____ the desk.
4 A Who can speak Spanish? I _____ read this menu.
   B Give _____ to me. I know some Spanish.
5 A Selina's class is at 8:00 p.m., but there _____ buses in the evening.
   B It's OK. I can drive _____ to the class.

3 Choose the correct options to complete the text.

A treehouse with a difference

If you want an unusual house, Jono Williams can ¹ *make / makes* one for you. He's an engineer, and he loves treehouses, but his new Skysphere is different – it's very small, and it's not ² *in / under* a tree!

What's in the Skysphere?
³ *There's / There are* a large bed, a TV, and ⁴ *any / some* shelves. There's even a refrigerator for drinks ⁵ *between / in* the sofa! The windows are very large, and Jono ⁶ *can / can't* see 360° around the house. There's Wi-Fi, and he can ⁷ *use / using* his smartphone to play music and change the lights.

What does Jono do there?
Jono meets his friends at the Skysphere. They love ⁸ *them / it* too. They like listening to music, and at night they can watch the stars.

Are there ⁹ *some / any* **problems with Jono's house?**
Only one … there ¹⁰ *'s no / are no* bathroom.

Vocabulary

1 Put the words in the box in the correct columns.

| museum   lamp   table   DVD player   remote control |
| head   teeth   park   chair   GPS   laptop   desk |
| police station   post office   face   foot |

Places in town	Electronic devices	Parts of the body	Furniture

2 Circle the word that is different. Explain your answers.

1 sink   bathtub   table   shower
2 ear   mouth   nose   hand
3 school   grocery store restaurant   café
4 bank   kitchen   bedroom   living room
5 chair   arm   refrigerator   closet
6 walking   reading   swimming   bike riding
7 sing   speak   travel   call
8 DVD player shelves   computer   GPS

3 Choose the correct options to complete the sentences.

1 My city has two _____.
   a closets   b hospitals   c bathrooms
2 What time does the bus _____ downtown?
   a arrive   b travel   c go out
3 Her _____ is long and brown.
   a eye   b hair   c mouth
4 There's a large _____ in the living room.
   a bathtub   b leg   c sofa
5 She always uses _____ to listen to music on the bus.
   a earphones b TV   c shelves
6 A Where's the _____? B It's in the car.
   a museum   b bathroom   c GPS
7 Is there any cheese in the _____?
   a shower   b refrigerator c DVR
8 On the weekend, I like _____ at the movie theater.
   a dancing   b sleeping   c watching movies

4 Complete the conversations with the words in the boxes.

| bedroom stove windows desk club cooking |

Ama Hi, Ed! How are you? Do you like your new apartment?
Ed No, not really. It's above a noisy ¹_____.
Ama Oh no! Is it big?
Ed No, it's very small. In the ²_____, there's only a bed and a ³_____, and there are no ⁴_____ in the bathroom.
Ama How's the kitchen? I know you like ⁵_____.
Ed It's dirty and the ⁶_____ is very old … but it's a good apartment.
Ama What's good about it?
Ed It's cheap!

| call station office speak drive stop |

Sam Excuse me. Do you ⁷_____ English?
Fran Yes, I do.
Sam Where's the bus ⁸_____?
Fran It's in front of the post ⁹_____, but there are no buses today.
Sam OK. Is there a train ¹⁰_____ near here?
Fran Yes, but it's a long walk. I can ¹¹_____ you there if you want.
Sam No thanks, I can ¹²_____ a taxi.

59

UNIT 7 All in the past

LANGUAGE simple past: *be* ■ celebrities

7A When they were young

1 Match the jobs in the box with pictures a–f.

musician   politician   movie director   writer   soccer player   fashion model

Go to Vocabulary practice: celebrities, page 123

2 In pairs, describe celebrities. Can your partner guess who it is?

A *She's a tennis player. She's American. She's very good!*   B *Is it Serena Williams?*

3 A Read the introduction of the text. Match the blue sign with one of the people a–e.

B Read the rest of the text. Match the other people with descriptions 1-4. Check their names on page 139 and write their names on the blue signs.

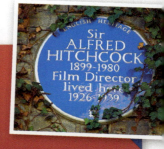

London's famous houses

London was home to lots of famous people from all over the world. Who were they and where were their houses? It's easy – just look for the blue signs on the buildings!

1869–1948 Lived here as a law student

1 He was a famous Indian politician, but he was also a student in London for three years. He was a vegetarian, and, in the 19th century, it wasn't easy to find good vegetarian food in the city.

1945–1981 Singer and musician Lived here 1972

2 In 1972, London was home to this Jamaican singer and his band. The musicians weren't famous then, but a year later their song *Stir It Up* was a big hit.

1890–1976 Writer Lived here 1934–1941

3 This British writer wasn't from London, but she was here for seven years. Her crime stories were very popular around the world, and you probably know her famous detective – Hercule Poirot.

1853–1890 Artist Lived here 1873–1874

4 This was the Dutch artist's home when he was 19 years old. He was in love with the owner's daughter, Eugenie. But was she interested in him? No, she wasn't!

simple past: *be* ■ celebrities   **LANGUAGE**   **7A**

4 A Complete the sentences with the words in the box. Check your answers in the text.

was (x2)   were (x2)   wasn't   weren't

1 Where _____ their houses?
2 He _____ a famous Indian politician.
3 It _____ easy to find good vegetarian food.
4 The musicians _____ famous then.
5 Her crime stories _____ very popular.
6 _____ she interested in him?

B Complete the rules. Then read the Grammar box.

1 The simple past forms of *is*/*'s not* = _____ / _____ .
2 The simple past forms of *are*/*'re not* = _____ / _____ .

Grammar   simple past: *be*

Affirmative:
He **was** a musician.
They **were** singers.

Negative:
I **wasn't** an actor.
You **weren't** famous.

Questions:
Was she a writer?
Were you happy?

Short answers:
Yes, she **was**.   No, she **wasn't**.
Yes, we **were**.   No, we **weren't**.

Go to Grammar practice: simple past: *be*, page 102

5 A ▶ 7.3   **Pronunciation:** *was/were* Listen and repeat the question and answer.
How are *was* and *were* pronounced?

A *Where were you yesterday?*   B *I was at work.*

B In pairs, ask and answer the question *Where were you …?* with the times in the boxes.
Pay attention to the pronunciation of *was* and *were*.

A *Where were you at 7:30 this morning?*   B *I was on the bus. I always go to work early. What about you?*
A *I was in bed!*

at 7:30 this morning | yesterday morning | yesterday at 2:00 p.m. | yesterday evening

Go to Communication practice: Student A page 139, Student B page 147

6 ▶ 7.4   Complete the sentences with the correct form of *was* or *were*. Listen and check.

When they were young

- Singer Justin Timberlake and actor Ryan Gosling [1]_____ hosts on a children's TV show when they [2]_____ young.

- In 1990, J.K. Rowling [3]_____ an English teacher in Portugal, but she [4]_____ happy there. Seven years later, she [5]_____ famous all over the world as the writer of the *Harry Potter* books.

- Actors and movie directors Matt Damon and Ben Affleck [6]_____ in school together, but they [7]_____ in the same class.

- Athlete Usain Bolt [8]_____ interested in cricket and soccer in school. His teachers [9]_____ surprised because he [10]_____ a very, very fast runner!

7 In pairs, ask and answer questions about when you were young. Use the ideas below.

A *What was the name of your first teacher?*   B *Mrs. Fuentes. She was really nice. What about you?*

1 What / the name of your first teacher?
2 / you a good student?
3 / you in a big class?
4 Who / your best friend?
5 What celebrities / popular when you / a child?
6 What movies / popular?
7 What / your favorite TV shows?
8 What / your favorite food?

Personal Best   Think of someone famous that you like. Write a paragraph about their life when they were young.

7 SKILLS LISTENING   listening for dates ■ linking consonants and vowels ■ months and ordinals

7B I was there in July

1 Order the months from 1–12.

- ☐ April
- ☐ August
- ☐ December
- ☐ February
- ☑ January (1)
- ☐ July
- ☐ June
- ☐ March
- ☐ May
- ☐ November
- ☐ October
- ☐ September

2 Look at the calendar. Match days a–f with dates 1–6.

1 May thirty-first _____
2 May twentieth _____
3 May twenty-eighth _____
4 May twelfth _____
5 May first _____
6 May third _____

Go to Vocabulary practice: months and ordinals, page 124

3 Ask and answer the questions in pairs.

1 What's the date today?
2 When's your birthday?
3 What's your favorite month?
4 When was the last national holiday?

4 A Look at the picture. What do you know about Shakespeare?

B Complete the text with the words in the box.

April   *Hamlet*   plays   writer

William Shakespeare was a famous British ¹_____ . He was born on ²_____ 26, 1564, and he died in April, 1616. His ³_____ are popular all over the world. They include *Romeo and Juliet*, ⁴_____ , and *Othello*.

5 ▶ 7.7 Watch or listen to the first part of *Learning Curve*. Are the sentences true (T) or false (F)?

1 Shakespeare's plays are only about British people. _____
2 The Globe Theatre was Shakespeare's first theater. _____
3 "Shakespeare in the Park" in New York is very expensive. _____
4 You can read Shakespeare's plays in 80 different languages. _____

Skill listening for dates

It's sometimes important to listen for specific years and months.
- Listen carefully because some months sound similar: Se*ptember*, *No*vember and De*cember*.
- Years are usually divided into two numbers: *1990 = nineteen ninety, 2010 = twenty ten*.
  For years after 2000, we sometimes use the whole number: *2009 = two thousand and nine*.
- We use ordinals to talk about centuries (100 years): *1900–1999 = the twentieth century*.

6 ▶ 7.7 Read the Skill box. Watch or listen again. Complete the texts with the correct information.

The Globe Theatre was Shakespeare's first theater. It was here in London during the ¹_____ and ²_____ centuries, from ³_____ to about ⁴_____ . This theater looks just like the old Globe.

Every year, from ⁵_____ to ⁶_____ , there's a Shakespeare festival in Central Park in New York City. It's called "Shakespeare in the Park." 1,800 people can see a Shakespeare play at the Delacorte Theater for free!

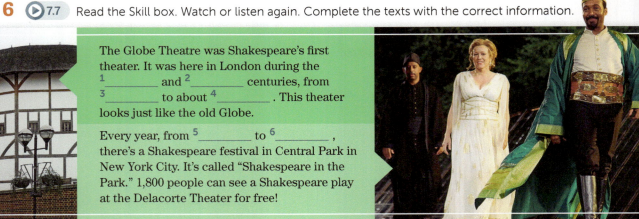

listening for dates ■ linking consonants and vowels ■ months and ordinals   **LISTENING**   SKILLS   **7B**

7 ▶ 7.8 Watch or listen to the rest of the show. Match the people with sentences 1–4.

Marty

Elizabeth and Henry

Zhang

1 This person likes plays about love. _____
2 This person works at a theater. _____
3 This person doesn't like Shakespeare. _____
4 This person likes plays about history. _____

8 ▶ 7.8 Watch or listen again. Answer the questions with months or years.
1 When does Marty come to New York? _____ and _____
2 When were Elizabeth and Henry in Cambridge? _____
3 When was *A Midsummer Night's Dream* in Beijing? _____
4 When was *Henry IV* at the Hong Kong Arts Festival? _____

9 Ask and answer the questions in pairs.

Do you ever go to the theater?   Which Shakespeare plays do you know?
Which types of plays do you like?   Do you like Shakespeare? Why/Why not?

10 ▶ 7.9 Listen to Penny's sentence and look at the linked words. Pay attention to how the sounds join together.

A lot͜ of people͜ are here͜ in the line for theater tickets.

Listening builder   linking consonants and vowels

When a word ends in a consonant sound, and the next word starts with a vowel sound, we usually link the sounds together.
Hamlet͜ is͜ about͜ a prince͜ in Denmark.
I'm͜ Elizabeth, and this͜ is my husband, Henry.
Sometimes the plays͜ are͜ in͜ English͜ and Chinese.

11 ▶ 7.10 Read the Listening builder. Then listen and complete the sentences.
1 Hi, my name's Lucas, _____ _____ _____ _____ .
2 In _____ _____ _____ _____ New York City for the first time.
3 The play _____ _____ _____ _____ king.
4 She was born on _____ _____ _____ , 1999.
5 I like *Hamlet*, but I _____ _____ _____ the story.

12 Look at the pictures. Discuss the questions in pairs.

1 When was the last time you were at a play/a movie theater/a concert?
2 Which play/movie/band was it?
3 Was it good? Why/Why not?

Personal Best   Write a description of your favorite play or movie. Where does it happen? What's it about?

7 LANGUAGE — simple past: regular verbs ■ time expressions

7C Famous decades

1 Match the decades in the box with a–f.

the nineties   the twenty-tens   the seventies   the two-thousands   the sixties   the eighties

a  b  c  d  e  f

2 Discuss the questions in pairs.

I was born in the eighties. What about you?

1 In which decade were you born?
2 Which decade has the best music and fashion, in your opinion?
3 Which was your favorite decade? Why?

3 ▶ 7.11 In pairs, complete the quiz with the years in the box. Listen and check.

1969   1973   1985   1991   2004   2012

The Decades Quiz

On February 4, ¹_____ , Mark Zuckerberg started Facebook from his bedroom in college. He wanted 500 people to join. Now, more than 1.5 billion people use it!

In ⁴_____ , Korean singer PSY danced *Gangnam Style* all over the world. The song was number 1 in 37 countries. Did you watch the video?

 On July 20, ²_____ , Neil Armstrong and Buzz Aldrin walked on the moon. 600 million people watched on TV or listened on the radio.

 On November 30, ⁵_____ , the U.S. and Norway played in the first Women's Soccer World Cup final in China. The result was a 2–1 win for the U.S.

In April ³_____ , Coca-Cola® tried a new recipe for their drink. People didn't like the flavor, and three months later, the original Coca-Cola was back in stores.

On April 3, ⁶_____ , Martin Cooper from Motorola called Joel Engel on the world's first cell phone. Joel quickly stopped the call because he wasn't happy. He worked for rival company AT&T!

4 Read the quiz again. Write the simple past form of verbs 1–8.

1 start _____   3 watch _____   5 dance _____   7 call _____
2 walk _____   4 try _____   6 play _____   8 stop _____

5 A Look at the verbs in exercise 4 again and complete the rules.

1 We usually add the letters ____ to verbs to make the simple past form.
2 If the verb ends in -e, we add the letter ____ to make the simple past form.
3 If the verb ends in consonant + y, we remove the y and add the letters ____ to make the simple past form.
4 If the verb ends in consonant + vowel + consonant, we double the last consonant and add ____ .

B Complete the sentences from the text to make the negative and question forms of the simple past. Does the main verb change form? Read the Grammar box.

1 People _____ like the flavor.   2 _____ you watch the video?

simple past: regular verbs ■ time expressions   LANGUAGE **7C**

📖 Grammar simple past: regular verbs

Affirmative:
600 million people **watched** on TV.
Coca-Cola **tried** a new recipe.

Negative:
They **didn't call** on a smartphone.
Brazil **didn't play** in the final.

Questions and short answers:
Did you **try** the new drink?
Yes, I **did**.   No, I **didn't**.

Go to Grammar practice: simple past: regular verbs, page 102

6 ▶ 7.13 Complete the text with the simple past form of the verbs in parentheses. Listen and check.

Were the nineties the best decade for movies?

My brother ¹_____ (study) movies in college, and he thinks the nineties were the best decade for movies. So last week, I ²_____ (decide) to watch the movie *Titanic* for the first time. It was in theaters 20 years ago, but I was only two then.
I ³_____ (love) it … but it's a sad story. It's about a real disaster that ⁴_____ (happen) in 1912 in the Atlantic Ocean. Thousands of people ⁵_____ (die) because the ship ⁶_____ (not carry) enough lifeboats.
After that, I ⁷_____ (want) to see more movies from the nineties. So, on the weekend, I ⁸_____ (watch) *Jurassic Park*, *Forrest Gump*, and *Pulp Fiction*. On Monday, it was *Toy Story*, and last night, I ⁹_____ (start) watching *The Matrix* … but I ¹⁰_____ (not finish) it because at 1:00 a.m. I ¹¹_____ (need) to go to bed. My brother was right – movies from the nineties are amazing!

7 Complete the time expressions with the words in the box. Check your answers in the text in exercise 6.

| in   ago   last (x2)   on (x2)   at |

1 20 years _____
2 _____ week
3 _____ 1912
4 _____ the weekend
5 _____ night
6 _____ Monday
7 _____ 1:00 a.m.

Go to Vocabulary practice: time expressions, page 124

8 A ▶ 7.15 **Pronunciation:** *-ed* endings Listen and repeat the sentences from the text.
Pay attention to the *-ed* endings in **bold**: /d/, /t/, and /ɪd/.

1 /d/   lov**ed**   I lov**ed** it.
2 /t/   watch**ed**   I watch**ed** *Jurassic Park*.
3 /ɪd/ need**ed**   I need**ed** to go to bed.

B ▶ 7.16 Write the verbs in the box in the correct columns. Listen, check, and repeat.

| danced   wanted   played   tried   walked   visited |

/d/	/t/	/ɪd/

Go to Communication practice: Student A page 139, Student B page 147

9 A In pairs, ask and answer the questions with the simple past form of the verbs. Write your partner's answers in the chart.

A *When did you last watch a movie on DVD?*
B *I watched a movie on DVD about a year ago.*

When did you last …	Answers
1 watch / a movie on DVD?	
2 study / for an exam?	
3 cook / chicken?	
4 play / a musical instrument?	
5 call / a friend on the phone?	

When was the last time you …	Answers
6 use / a computer?	
7 dance / with friends?	
8 relax / at home?	
9 talk / to a neighbor?	
10 listen / to the radio?	

B Tell the class about your partner.

Marco watched a movie on DVD about a year ago.

  Choose six different time expressions and write a true simple past sentence for each one.

65

7 SKILLS WRITING writing informal e-mails ■ sequencers

7D A weekend away

1 In pairs, order the pictures from 1–6 to make a story about Elena and her father's trip to Boston.

2 Read Elena's e-mail and check the order of the pictures in exercise 1.

To: Becky Stewart
Subject: My weekend

Hi Becky,
How are things? I hope you're well.
Did I tell you about last weekend? I visited my sister Hannah. She lives in Boston now. I wanted to go on my own … but Dad decided to come with me!
We traveled by train on Saturday. We arrived in Boston and Hannah was at the train station. In the afternoon, we explored the city. First, we walked around one of the universities. It was beautiful, but Dad stopped to take hundreds of pictures! Then we visited an art gallery. Dad studied every painting and looked at every sculpture – we were there for hours! After that, Hannah and I wanted to go shopping, but Dad wanted to visit a museum. It was so boring!
It was a disaster! This weekend, I want to stay at home, or go away without Dad!
See you soon.
Elena

---

3 A Read the e-mail again. Are the sentences true (T) or false (F)?

1 Elena and her dad traveled to Boston. _____
2 They stayed in Boston for a week. _____
3 Elena's dad didn't like the university. _____
4 They explored the university on foot. _____
5 They didn't stay in the art gallery for a long time. _____
6 Hannah and Elena didn't want to visit the museum. _____

B Look at the e-mail again and answer the questions. Then read the Skill box.

1 How does Elena start her e-mail?
2 How does she ask how her friend is?
3 How does she introduce her news?
4 How does she finish her e-mail?

Skill writing informal e-mails

We write informal e-mails to friends and people we know well.
- Start the e-mail in a friendly way: *Hi …, Hello …*
- Ask about the person: *How are you? How are things? I hope you're well.*
- Say why you are writing: *Did I tell you about …? I wanted to tell/ask you …*
- Finish the e-mail in a friendly way: *See you soon, Bye for now, See you later.*

writing informal e-mails ■ sequencers **WRITING** **SKILLS** **7D**

4 Complete the e-mail with the words in the box.

hope   how   hello   tell   now

To: George Hawkins
Subject: Fantastic weekend

¹_____ George,
²_____ are you? I ³_____ you and the family are well.
I wanted to ⁴_____ you about last weekend. My daughter Elena and I traveled to Boston. My other daughter, Hannah, moved there a few months ago, so we stayed with her.
On Saturday, we walked into town. First, we explored one of the universities. It was very interesting. Elena loved all the old buildings! Then we visited an art gallery. We were there for hours – the girls didn't want to leave! After that, we looked around the museum. I was pretty tired, but the girls really enjoyed it. It was a great weekend. I think Elena wants to do it again soon.
Bye for ⁵_____ .
Frank

5 Discuss the questions in pairs.
1 Who is Frank?
2 What differences are there between Frank and Elena's e-mails?
3 Do you enjoy visiting art galleries and museums? Why/Why not?

6 Order sentences a–c from 1–3. Check your answers in the e-mail in exercise 4.
a ☐ After that, we looked around the museum.
b ☐ First, we explored the university.
c ☐ Then we visited an art gallery.

Text builder | **sequencers**

We can show the order of events with *First*, *Then*, and *After that*:
First, we walked into town. *Then* we visited the university. *After that*, we explored the downtown area.

Look! We usually use a comma after *First* and *After that*.

7 Read the Text builder. Then write sentences in the simple past with sequencers.
First, we listened to some music. Then we cooked dinner …
1 We / listen to / some music. We / cook / dinner. We / watch / a movie.
2 She / visit / her sister. She / call / her mom. She / talk to / her dad.
3 I / walk to / my friend's house. We / study / English together. We / play / soccer.

8 A PREPARE Think of a weekend when you were somewhere interesting. Make notes about what happened. Think about:
- where you traveled to
- how you traveled
- who was with you
- where you stayed
- the places that you visited
- if you enjoyed it

Use these regular verbs to help you:

visit   travel   play   walk   watch   listen to   wait   love
cook   explore   stay   talk   enjoy   need   want   try

B PRACTICE Write an e-mail to a friend about your weekend. Use the Skill box and Text builder to help you.

C PERSONAL BEST Exchange e-mails with your partner. Does your partner use the simple past correctly? Can you correct any mistakes?

Personal Best Write about a day when you visited a lot of places, like Elena's day in Boston. 67

UNIT 8

Travel

LANGUAGE   simple past: irregular verbs ■ travel verbs

8A Incredible trips

1 Complete the sentences with the verbs in the box.

> get lost   book   fly   miss   ride   take

1 Some of my friends _____ motorcycles to work.

3 I sometimes _____ the bus because I get up late.

5 I never _____ because I don't like it!

2 I always _____ train tickets early to get a good price.

4 If I go out at night, I usually _____ a taxi home.

6 I often _____ in a new town.

Go to Vocabulary practice: travel verbs, page 125

2 In pairs, say the sentences in exercise 1. Decide if they are true or false for your partner.

A *Some of my friends ride motorcycles to work.*   B *False.*
A *You're right. All my friends drive to work.*

3 Look at the title and the picture. In pairs, guess what the story is about. Read the text and check.

Around the world *for love*

In January 2001, Ian Johnstone from Yorkshire in the UK went to work in Australia for a year, but his girlfriend Amy stayed at home. It was difficult to be so far away from her and after six months, Ian planned to visit her. He wanted to ask her to marry him, but he didn't tell her about his plans … it was a surprise visit!

Ian booked a flight, and in July he flew from Sydney to London, with a layover in Singapore. But he didn't know about Amy's plans. She also wanted to surprise Ian with a visit, and at that exact moment, she was also on a plane … to Australia!

When Ian arrived in London, he bought some flowers and took the train to Yorkshire. Amy wasn't at home, so Ian waited for her. At the same time, Amy arrived at Ian's apartment in Sydney. When his roommate told her that Ian was 17,000 kilometers miles away in England, Amy thought that it was a joke!

It wasn't possible for Ian or Amy to change their tickets, so they didn't see each other. But the story had a happy ending. Ian called Amy and asked her to marry him. And what did she say? She said "yes," of course!

68

simple past: irregular verbs ∎ travel verbs **LANGUAGE** **8A**

4 Are the sentences true (T) or false (F)? Read the text again and check.

1 Ian went to Australia with Amy. _____
2 He wanted to see his girlfriend. _____
3 Amy lived in London. _____
4 She traveled to Australia to see Ian. _____
5 They changed their tickets. _____
6 Amy didn't want to marry Ian. _____

5 **A** Look at the simple past verbs in **bold** in the sentence from the text. Which verb is regular and which is irregular?

Ian **booked** a flight, and in July he **flew** from Sydney to London.

B Find the simple past form of the irregular verbs in the text. Then read the Grammar box.

1 go _____ 2 fly _____ 3 buy _____ 4 take _____ 5 think _____ 6 say _____

📖 **Grammar** | **simple past: irregular verbs**

Affirmative:	**Negative:**	**Questions:**	**Short answers:**
Ian **went** to work in Australia.	Ian **didn't go** to work in Singapore.	**Did** Ian **go** home?	Yes, he **did**.
He **flew** to London.	He **didn't fly** to Sydney.	**Did** he **fly** alone?	No, he **didn't**.
He **bought** some flowers.	He **didn't buy** chocolate.	**Did** he **buy** a ring?	

Personal Best

Go to Grammar practice: simple past: irregular verbs, page 103

6 Complete the text with the simple past form of the verbs in parentheses.

Around the world – on foot! 👣 👣 👣 👣

This is Jean Béliveau, a Canadian who walked around the world, through 64 countries in 11 years!

When ¹_____ he _____ (leave)?
Jean ²_____ (leave) his home on August 18, 2000, and he ³_____ (not get) home until 2011.
His wife, Luce, ⁴_____ (not go) with him, but she ⁵_____ (fly) to meet him eleven times.
Where ⁶_____ he _____ (sleep)?
He ⁷_____ (sleep) in people's homes, parks, schools, hospitals – and even in a police station!
People also ⁸_____ (buy) him food and drink.
Why ⁹_____ he _____ (do) it?
He ¹⁰_____ (do) it because he wanted people to know about children's lives in other countries.

7 **A** ▶8.3 **Pronunciation:** irregular simple past verbs Listen and repeat the simple past verbs. Pay attention to the vowel sounds /ɑ/, /ɔ/ and /ow/.

1 /ɑ/ got lost 2 /ɔ/ bought thought 3 /ow/ rode drove

B ▶8.4 Underline the words in the sentences with the same vowel sounds. Listen, check, and repeat.

1 I got on the bus. 3 I rode home on my bike. 5 She thought it was her ball.
2 We all bought a ticket. 4 He lost his job. 6 She drove to my home.

Go to Communication practice: Student A page 140, Student B page 148

8 **A** ▶8.5 Read Leanne's plans for a vacation in California last summer. Then listen and correct the information with what really happened.

B In pairs, make sentences about Leanne's trip.

She didn't fly from Tampa. She flew from Orlando.

9 Think about a vacation or trip. In pairs, ask and answer the questions in the boxes.

My trip to California

July 24: fly from Tampa to San Diego
July 30: take bus to Los Angeles
August 5: sail to Catalina Island
August 10: take taxi to San Francisco and drive home
Activities: eat local food, swim in the ocean, take pictures … fall in love?

Where did you go? How did you travel? What did you do?
When did you go? Who did you go with? Did you have a good time?

Personal Best | Write about your partner's vacation or trip from exercise 9.

69

8 SKILLS READING understanding the main idea ■ modifiers ■ weather and seasons

8B Crazy weather!

1 Match the weather phrases in the box with pictures a–d on page 71.

> It's cold.   It's sunny.   It's raining.   It's windy.

Go to Vocabulary practice: weather and seasons, page 126

2 In pairs, talk about the seasons in your country. Use *love/like/don't like/hate*.
I don't like the fall because it rains, and it's cold and windy.

> **Skill** understanding the main idea
>
> When you see a text for the first time, try to understand the main idea quickly.
> - Look at the title and pictures.
> - Read the first line of each paragraph.
> - Use this information to understand what the text is about.

3 **A** Read the Skill box. Then read the title and the highlighted sentences on page 71. Check (✓) the main idea.
  a Robbie had lots of problems with transportation in Germany. ☐
  b Robbie went on vacation, and the weather changed a lot. ☐
  c Robbie was in Berlin in the summer, but it snowed all week. ☐
  d Robbie didn't like the weather in Germany, so he went to Ireland. ☐

  B Read the whole text and check.

4 Are the sentences true (T) or false (F)? Read the text again and check.
  1 Robbie went to Berlin with his girlfriend. ___
  2 They had ice cream in Viktoria Park. ___
  3 They waited for a train for three hours. ___
  4 It rained at the Television Tower. ___
  5 They didn't go to the concert because it snowed. ___
  6 They arrived at the airport late and missed the flight. ___

5 Match the halves to make sentences from the text. Do the modifiers in **bold** come before or after the adjectives?
  1 When we got off the plane, it was **very**   a cold.
  2 When we got to the park, it was **pretty**   b good.
  3 And in the afternoon, it was **really**   c windy.
  4 The views were**n't very**   d hot and sunny.

> **Text builder** modifiers
>
> We use modifiers before an adjective to make the meaning stronger or less strong:
> really/very   It was **really** sunny. The movie was **very** exciting.
> pretty   The museum was **pretty** interesting.
> not very   The food was**n't very** good.

6 Read the Text builder. Then write sentences with the words and a modifier.
The weather today is very hot.
  1 the weather today / hot
  2 the *Star Wars* movies / exciting
  3 I think English / difficult
  4 public transportation in my country / expensive
  5 my street / noisy
  6 people in my city / friendly

7 In pairs, talk about your last trip or vacation. What was the weather like?
Last year, I visited Morocco. It was very hot and sunny in the day, and really cold at night.

understanding the main idea ■ modifiers ■ weather and seasons **READING** SKILLS 8B

Travel news

Four Seasons In One Week

Robbie Irwin

Monday, March 12

My girlfriend and I arrived in Berlin today on vacation. We thought Germany was cold in March, so we only brought winter clothes, but we had a surprise. When we got off the plane, it was very hot and sunny! So, this afternoon, we went shopping and bought shorts and T-shirts and walked around downtown. I even had ice cream!

Wednesday, March 14

Today, we decided to visit Viktoria Park, but the weather changed. It was warm when we left the hotel, so we wore our new shorts and T-shirts. But when we got to the park, it was pretty cold. And in the afternoon, it was really windy. We decided to visit Museum Island, so we took a train back into the city … but a tree fell on the tracks, and we didn't move for three hours! After that, we went back to the hotel, changed our clothes, and had dinner in a restaurant.

Thursday, March 15

The weather here is crazy – this morning it was sunny again! We decided to visit the famous Television Tower. It's over a thousand feet high and I wanted to take some pictures of the city. But when we got to the top of the tower, it was cloudy and it started to rain – the views weren't very good. We bought some umbrellas and went to see a concert. When we came out – guess what? It was warm and sunny again!

Saturday, March 17

I can't believe it – it's 11:00 p.m. and we're still in Berlin Airport! It's really cold, and it snowed all day. We took a taxi to the airport, and when we arrived, we saw that there were no flights. The next flight is tomorrow morning at 7:00 a.m.

Sunday, March 18

Finally, we're back home in Ireland. We had bad luck with the weather, but we had a great trip, and we loved Berlin.

Personal Best Write a paragraph about the weather in your town or city in different seasons.

8 LANGUAGE *there was/were* ■ nature

8C Then and now

1 Match the words in the box with the parts of the picture 1–6.

| sky field forest mountain river tree |

1 _____   4 _____
2 _____   5 _____
3 _____   6 _____

Go to Vocabulary practice: nature, page 127

2 Discuss the questions in pairs.
  1 Which country is the picture in exercise 1?
  2 What nature can you see out of the window?
  3 Do you prefer beaches, mountains, or forests? Why?

3 Read the introduction to a radio show. Answer the questions.
  1 How many people live in Shenzhen? _____
  2 Where does Liu Jiang live now? _____
  3 What's her job? _____
  4 When was she last in Shenzhen? _____

Then and Now:
Shenzhen, China

In the 1970s, Shenzhen was a small fishing town. Today, it is an enormous city of 12 million people. Liu Jiang, a Chinese-American writer from Chicago, lived in Shenzhen as a child. Listen as she returns to the city for the first time in 30 years.

Sunday, June 28, 9:00 p.m.   Radio 7

4 ▶8.8 Listen to the radio show. Check (✓) the things that Shenzhen had 30 years ago and has today.

	Fields	Forest	Tall buildings	River	Train station	Airport	College
Shenzhen 30 years ago							
Shenzhen today							

5 A ▶8.8 Match the halves to make sentences and questions. Listen again and check.

1 **There were** fields   a or buses?
2 **There was** a forest   b here before.
3 **There were no** cars   c – everyone had bikes.
4 **Was there** public transportation d to travel around the country?
5 **Were there** any trains   e where we played.
6 **There was no** college   f around the town.

B Look at the words in **bold** in sentences 1–6 again. Choose the correct options to complete the rules. Then read the Grammar box.

1 We use *there was* and *there were* to talk about *the present / the past*.
2 We use *there was* and *there was no* with *singular / plural* nouns.
3 We use *there were* and *there were no* with *singular / plural* nouns.

72

there was/were ■ nature **LANGUAGE 8C**

  Grammar *there was/were*

Affirmative:	Negative:	Questions	Short answers:
There was a train station.	There was no airport.	Was there a college?	Yes, there was. No, there wasn't.
There were lots of trees.	There were no cars. / There weren't any cars.	Were there any stores?	Yes, there were. No, there weren't.

Go to Grammar practice: *there was/were*, page 103

6 Complete the text with the correct forms of *there was/were*.

This is Pompeii in Italy. In A.D. 79, a volcano destroyed the city. But what was life like for the 20,000 people that lived there before?
¹_____ about 200 cafés in the town. They sold eggs, cheese, bread, and fruit. ²_____ also a market.
Children attended class outside or at home, so ³_____ any school buildings. ⁴_____ some doctors, but ⁵_____ no hospital.
⁶_____ a big amphitheater, where ⁷_____ plays and concerts. And of course, ⁸_____ gladiators!

7 A ▶ 8.10 **Pronunciation: sentence stress** Listen and repeat the questions and short answers. Pay attention to the underlined stressed words.

1 Was there a <u>train</u> <u>station</u>?   Yes, there <u>was</u>.
2 Was there an <u>airport</u>?   No, there <u>wasn't</u>.
3 Were there any <u>trees</u>?   Yes, there <u>were</u>.
4 Were there any <u>cars</u>?   No, there <u>weren't</u>.

B ▶ 8.11 In pairs, ask and answer questions 1–4 about Pompeii. Remember to stress the correct words. Listen, check, and repeat.

1 Were there any cafés?
2 Was there a market?
3 Were there any school buildings?
4 Was there a hospital?

Go to Communication practice: Student A page 140, Student B page 148

8 In pairs, look at the pictures and talk about Oxford Street in London in the past. Use the words in the box and your own ideas.

buses   road   stores   horses and carriages   tall buildings   bus stops   street lights   taxis

There were no buses in the 19th century.

Oxford Street, 19th century   Oxford Street, now

9 How is your town or city different from the past? In pairs, talk about the differences.

There was a movie theater on Panama Street, but now there's a grocery store.

Personal Best   Write about where you lived when you were a child.

73

8 SKILLS SPEAKING starting and ending a phone call at work ■ buying a ticket

8D A trip to Canada

1 Ask and answer the questions in pairs.

1 Why do you usually travel?
  a for work or study   b to visit friends or family   c to go on vacation   d other
2 How do you prefer to travel? Why?
  a to take the train   b to fly   c to drive   d other
3 How do you usually book your tickets when you travel?
  a online   b on the phone   c at a travel agent's   d other

2 A ▶ 8.12 Watch or listen to the first part of *Learning Curve*. Answer the questions.

1 Why does Marc want to travel?
2 How does he prefer to travel?
3 How does he book the tickets?

B ▶ 8.12 Are the sentences true (T) or false (F)? Watch or listen again, and check.

1 Marc works with technology. ____
2 He never buys tickets online. ____
3 He loves flying. ____
4 Clarisse is Marc's friend. ____
5 It's hot and sunny in California. ____
6 The trip to Montreal takes 11 hours. ____

3 ▶ 8.13 Complete the questions with the words in the box. Listen and check.

arrive how leave when return

1 **Clarisse** _____ do you want to leave?
  Marc March 11.
2 **Clarisse** When would you like to _____?
  Marc March 21.
3 **Marc** What time does the train _____?
  Clarisse The train leaves from New York at 8:15 a.m.
4 **Marc** And when does it _____ in Montreal?
  Clarisse 7:11 p.m.
5 **Marc** So, _____ much is it?
  Clarisse It's $138 for a round-trip ticket.

Conversation builder | buying a ticket

Customer:
I'd like a one-way/round-trip ticket to ...
What time does the train/bus/flight leave?
What time/When does it arrive?
How much is it?

Assistant:
What kind of ticket would you like?
Would you like a one-way or round-trip ticket?
When do you want to return/leave?
It's ... for a one-way/round-trip ticket.

4 Read the Conversation builder. Then, in pairs, make conversations to buy the tickets.

A *I'd like a one-way ticket to San Diego, please.*   **B** *When would you like to leave?*

Ticket type: ONE-WAY
Adults: ONE
From: LOS ANGELES
To: SAN DIEGO
Date: FEB 8
Time: 9:55 a.m.
Arrival: 12:54 p.m.
Price: $37.00

OUTBOUND
Flight: AA 1503
Departing from: Chicago O'Hare
December 4, 8:25 a.m.
Arriving at: Cancún
December 4, 1:06 p.m.

RETURN
Flight: AA 2348
Departing from: Cancún
December 18, 2:00 p.m.
Arriving at: Chicago O'Hare
December 18, 4:57 p.m.

Price: $382.00

starting and ending a phone call at work ■ buying a ticket   **SPEAKING**   **SKILLS** **8D**

5 A ▶ 8.14 Watch or listen to the second part of the show. Do you think Marc enjoyed his trip? Why/Why not?

B ▶ 8.14 Choose the correct options to complete the sentences. Watch or listen again, and check.

1 Marc asks Clarisse about ____.
   a places to eat   b places to stay
   c public transportation
2 The Wi-Fi in Montreal's not good when ____.
   a it snows   b it rains   c it's windy
3 On his trip, Marc helped people with their ____.
   a coffee and sandwiches   b French   c Wi-Fi

6 ▶ 8.15 Listen to the phrases from the conversations. Are they for starting or ending a phone call?

1 Hello, *Bon Voyage Travel*. This is Clarisse.
2 Thanks. Goodbye.
3 Hello, my name is Marc Kim. I'm Penny's friend.
4 Thanks for calling.

Skill starting and ending a phone call at work

When you speak on the telephone, remember to give important information and be polite.
- When you answer the phone, say *Hello* and identify yourself or your company: *Hello, Learning Curve. Hello, this is Clarisse.*
- When you call someone, say who you are: *Hello, this is ... , My name's ...*
- When the conversation finishes, thank the person who called and say goodbye: *Thanks for calling. Thanks for your call.*

7 ▶ 8.16 Complete the conversations with the missing words. Listen and check.

Brad   Hello, *Easy Travel*. Brad ¹_____.
Jenny Hi, ²_____ is Jenny Foster. I'd like a one-way ticket to Seoul from Sydney, please.
...
Brad   OK, Jenny. You leave on June 15 at 08:15 and you arrive in Seoul at 17:05.
Jenny Thanks very much.
Brad   You're welcome. Thanks for your ³_____.
Jenny ⁴_____.

Go to Communication practice: Student A page 140, Student B page 148

8 A PREPARE Choose a type of transportation and write down the information.

train

bus

plane

ferry

- where you want to go
- what type of ticket you want
- when you want to leave
- if/when you want to return

B PRACTICE Sit back-to-back with a partner. Act out a telephone call to buy a ticket. Then switch roles.

C PERSONAL BEST Listen to another pair. Write down three things that they do well.

Personal Best Write a conversation between a customer and a travel agent about a new trip.

7 and 8 REVIEW and PRACTICE

Grammar

1 Choose the correct options to complete the questions and sentences.

1 Where _____ last night?
  a you were
  b were you
  c you was

2 Our taxi driver _____ very friendly.
  a wasn't
  b not was
  c weren't

3 She _____ work at 7:00 p.m. last night.
  a did finish
  b finishes
  c finished

4 _____ soccer last weekend?
  a Did you play
  b You did play
  c You played

5 They _____ to Oslo for a meeting.
  a did fly
  b flied
  c flew

6 We had a map, so we _____ lost .
  a didn't get
  b didn't got
  c not got

7 _____ a restaurant in your hotel?
  a There was
  b Was there
  c Were there

8 _____ two police officers in the street last night.
  a There was
  b They were
  c There were

2 Rewrite the questions and sentences in the simple past.

1 Does she play tennis with Laura?
  _____ last weekend?

2 There are two eggs in the refrigerator.
  _____ last night.

3 I don't have time for breakfast.
  _____ this morning.

4 I ride my bike to work.
  _____ yesterday.

5 Do you go to the gym?
  _____ last Saturday?

6 He gets on the 8:00 a.m. train.
  _____ yesterday.

3 Complete the text with the simple past form of the verbs in parentheses.

Birds for friends

In many countries, people give food to birds in parks or in their yards. But Gabi Mann from Seattle in the U.S. has a very special relationship with the birds in her neighborhood – they bring *her* gifts!
The story ¹_____ (start) when Gabi ²_____ (be) four years old. She ³_____ (have) some food in the car and when she ⁴_____ (get out), the food fell on the ground. There ⁵_____ (be) a crow near the car and it ⁶_____ (fly) down to eat the food. After that, Gabi ⁷_____ (not eat) all of her lunch at school. Instead, she kept some and ⁸_____ (give) it to the birds on the way home. In 2013, she ⁹_____ (help) more birds and put food and water in the yard every morning. One day, the crows started bringing things like buttons, rocks, small pieces of metal or plastic, and even jewelry for Gabi. ¹⁰_____ they _____ (want) to say "thank you" to her? Gabi thinks so. She collects these "gifts" and she now has more than 100. Her favorite is a metal heart. "It shows me how much they love me," she says.

Vocabulary

1 Put the words in the box in the correct columns.

summer April cold field fifth fall first flower
grass hot March May mountain winter
ninth October second spring warm wet

Months	Ordinal numbers	Weather	Nature	Seasons

REVIEW and PRACTICE 7 and 8

2 Circle the word that is different. Explain your answers.

1	artist	musician	winter	dancer
2	week	rain	month	year
3	beach	dry	ocean	river
4	spring	summer	fall	windy
5	snow	ride	sail	fly
6	foggy	sunny	sky	cloudy
7	forest	sixth	third	fourth
8	king	queen	tree	politician

3 Choose the correct options to complete the sentences.

1 The summer in India is very _____ and wet.
   a hot   **b** sun   **c** cold

2 My sister _____ the train at King Street Station.
   a gets on   **b** gets in   **c** gets out

3 Don't _____ your bus! It leaves in five minutes.
   a take   **b** miss   **c** get lost

4 There are lots of big trees in this _____ .
   a flower   **b** foggy   **c** forest

5 Did you _____ your ticket to New York yesterday?
   a fly   **b** book   **c** sail

6 He _____ of the car at the police station.
   a got out   **b** got off   **c** got on

7 The _____ played the piano very well.
   a musician   **b** athlete   **c** dancer

8 It was a beautiful day, so we _____ to the park.
   a walked   **b** watched   **c** worked

9 With my smartphone, I never _____ in a new city.
   a miss   **b** get out   **c** get lost

10 You can't swim in the _____ . It's very dangerous.
   a river   **b** field   **c** sky

4 Complete the sentences with the words in the box.

> ago   6:00   at   summer   in (x2)   Friday
> last   on (x2)   yesterday   July

1 I went to Greece _____ year on vacation.

2 Did you meet your friends on _____ ?

3 He started work _____ 7:00 this morning.

4 We usually go shopping _____ Saturday.

5 We can take the train at _____ .

6 His birthday is _____ June.

7 He started a new job two weeks _____ .

8 _____ fourth is a national holiday.

9 I played tennis with my brother _____ .

10 What did you do _____ the weekend?

11 She lived in Bogotá _____ 2016.

12 We didn't go on vacation in the _____ .

Personal Best

Lesson 7A
Name five celebrities with different jobs.

Lesson 8A
List five irregular verbs and their simple past forms.

Lesson 7A
Write where you were on two different days last week.

Lesson 8B
Describe the weather in your favorite season.

Lesson 7B
Write the birthdays of four friends or family members.

Lesson 8B
Write three sentences with *very, pretty,* and *really,* and an adjective.

Lesson 7C
Write three sentences beginning *Last year …, Two years ago …,* and *Yesterday … .*

Lesson 8C
Name five things from nature you can see out of the window.

Lesson 7C
List five regular verbs and their simple past forms.

Lesson 8C
Write two sentences about your home as a child. Use *There was …* and *There were … .*

Lesson 7D
Describe what you did yesterday with *First, Then,* and *After that.*

Lesson 8D
Write three sentences for buying a train ticket.

77

UNIT 9 Shopping

LANGUAGE present continuous ■ clothes

9A Street style

1 Match the words in the box with the clothes in the picture.

| belt   jeans   jacket   T-shirt   hat |

1 _____ 2 _____ 3 _____ 4 _____ 5 _____

Go to Vocabulary practice: clothes, page 128

2 Discuss the questions in pairs.
  1 What do you usually wear …
    a at home?   b at work/in class?   c on vacation?
  2 Where do you usually buy your clothes? What's your favorite store?
  3 Do you buy used clothing? Why/Why not?

3 Read the text and answer the questions.
  1 Where is Sukanya from?
  2 What type of clothes does she wear?
  3 Why does she buy these clothes?
  4 Where does she take Mark?

Fashion Diary with Mark Ashcroft

This week, I'm in Thailand with local fashion blogger Sukanya Tanasan. Sukanya only wears used clothing, but she looks amazing!

"There are some great places to buy clothes in Bangkok," she says. "If I need a new dress, a T-shirt, or shoes, I always go to the markets. You can find really cool clothes there, and they're cheap too!"

Today, Sukanya takes me to the Chatuchak market in Bangkok on a shopping trip.

▶ PLAY   ⬇ DOWNLOAD

4 ▶9.2 Listen and check (✓) the things Sukanya buys.
T-shirt ☐ dress ☐ shoes ☐ hat ☐ skirt ☐

5 A ▶9.2 Complete the sentences with the words in the box. Listen again and check.

| getting   buying   taking   eating   leaving   doing |

1 We're _____ the train to Chatuchak market.
2 A lot of people are _____ out here.
3 She's _____ the dress!
4 What's this man _____ ?
5 Sukanya, you're not _____ the rice!
6 We're _____ the market now.

B Look at sentences 1–6 again and answer the questions. Then read the Grammar box.
  1 What are the sentences about? *things happening now / regular events*
  2 Which three letters are at the end of the main verbs? _____
  3 Which verb do we use before the main verb? *be / do*

present continuous ■ clothes   LANGUAGE 9A

  Grammar present continuous

Things that are happening now

Affirmative:
I**'m going** to the market.
We**'re getting off** the bus.

Negative:
She**'s not having** a drink.
They**'re not wearing** glasses.

Questions and short answers:
Are you **working** today?
Yes, I **am**.   No, I**'m not**.

Go to Grammar practice: present continuous, page 104

6 Complete the phone messages with the present continuous form of the verbs in parentheses.

7 A ▶9.4 **Pronunciation:** -*ing* endings Listen and repeat. Pay attention to the /ɪŋ/ sound in **bold**.

com**ing** go**ing** do**ing** runn**ing** wait**ing** stay**ing**

B ▶9.5 Say the questions and sentences. Then listen, check and repeat.

1 Where are you going?
2 She's running for her bus.
3 I'm not doing any work.
4 Are you staying?
5 He's coming to the café.
6 We're waiting for a taxi.

Go to Communication practice: Student A page 150, Student B page 149

8 In pairs, ask and answer the question *What is/are ... doing?* about the people in the pictures.

A *What's David doing?*
B *I think he's having lunch in a restaurant.*

Jorge ● online

Hi, Jorge, what ¹_____ you _____ (do)?
I ²_____ (go) downtown with my sister.   11:35

Cool! I'm there too.   11:36

Do you want to meet for a coffee in 30 mins? The café on Bridge Street?   11:36

11:37

I ³_____ (sit) next to the window. My sister ⁴_____ (not/stay). She needs to buy a new dress. Are you here?   12:05

I ⁵_____ (get) a coffee.
Do you want one?   12:10

⁶_____ you _____ (come) ?!   12:19

I'm sorry. My battery died. I ⁷_____ (run) to the café now.   12:25

Too late. We ⁸_____ (wait) for the bus home.   12:23   12:26

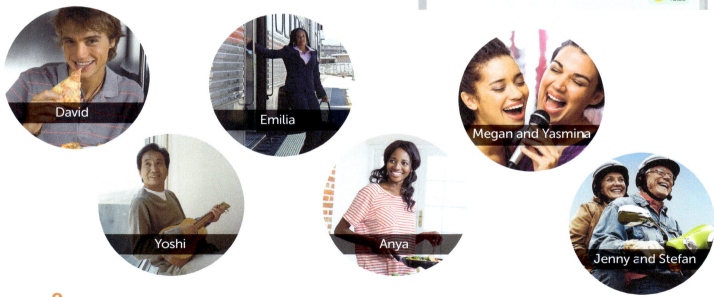

David   Emilia   Megan and Yasmina   Yoshi   Anya   Jenny and Stefan

9 In pairs, describe a classmate. Your partner guesses the person.

A *She's wearing a blue dress, and she's sitting next to Leon.*
B *Is it Malika?*
A *Yes, it is!*

Personal Best Think of six people you know. Write sentences about what they're doing at the moment.   79

9 SKILLS LISTENING identifying key points ■ filler words ■ feelings

9B How do you feel?

1 Match the words in the box with pictures a–f.

angry calm excited hungry thirsty tired

Go to Vocabulary practice: feelings, page 129

2 ▶ 9.7 Complete the text with four feelings from exercise 1. Listen and check.

Colors and feelings

Colors can sometimes change how we feel. For example, orange can make us feel happy and ¹_____ . A lot of restaurants, for example McDonald's and KFC, use red because it can make us feel ²_____ . Offices often use blue because it makes us ³_____ . But gray's not a popular color for offices because it can make us feel sad or ⁴_____ .

3 A Look at the picture of Ethan. How does his shirt make you feel?

B ▶ 9.8 Match the colors in the box with sentences 1–4. Watch or listen to the first part of *Learning Curve* and check.

orange blue white black yellow

1 Doctors often wear this color.   _____
2 Firefighters usually wear these colors.   _____ or _____
3 The police in the U.S. wear this color.   _____
4 People wear this color when they're sad.   _____

> **Skill   identifying key points**
>
> **When people speak, try to listen for the important things they say.**
> • We often emphasize or repeat the most important ideas.
> • We sometimes give examples or more information.

4 ▶ 9.8 Read the Skill box. Then watch or listen again. Check (✓) the **two** key points Ethan talks about.

a Colors can change how we feel. ☐
b Colors are important in festivals all around the world. ☐
c Orange is a popular color for clothes. ☐
d Workers sometimes wear uniforms of the same color. ☐

5 Discuss the questions in pairs.

1 Do you wear a uniform for work?
2 Did you wear a uniform at school?
3 What colors are/were the uniforms?
4 How do/did they make you feel?

identifying key points ■ filler words ■ feelings **LISTENING** **SKILLS** **9B**

6 ▶ 9.9 Watch or listen to the rest of the show. Match the feelings in the box with the people.

bored   excited   scared   hungry   thirsty

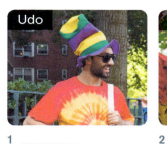   

Udo   Akiko   Penny   Bob

1 _____   2 _____   3 _____   4 _____ and _____

7 ▶ 9.9 Watch or listen again. Choose the correct options to complete the key points.
1 Udo _____ .
   a makes his own clothes   b buys expensive clothes   c only wears bright colors
2 Akiko _____ .
   a doesn't like *Learning Curve*   b doesn't like Ethan's shirt   c is late for class
3 Bob _____ .
   a loves the color yellow   b wears a uniform for work   c wants to eat something

8 Ask and answer the questions in the boxes.

What are you wearing today?   What colors are the clothes?   How do they make you feel?

9 ▶ 9.10 Read the two extracts. Can you understand them without the missing words? Listen and write the missing words.

1 _____ Penny, what are people wearing today? Do you see a lot of colors on the streets of New York?

2 _____ , people are leaving work at the moment. Let's see what they're wearing.

Listening builder   filler words

When people speak, they often say short words while they are thinking of what to say. You can ignore these words – they don't really mean anything.
So, what are you, *uh*, wearing today?
Well, I'm wearing blue jeans and, *um*, this red T-shirt.

10 ▶ 9.11 Read the Listening builder. Then listen to the description of the photo. Check (✓) the sentences the speaker says.
1 a This photo is of a young girl in a school. ☐
   b In this photo, there's a young girl at school. ☐
   c The photo shows a young girl in school. ☐
2 a And she's wearing a gray uniform and glasses. ☐
   b And she has a long gray uniform and glasses. ☐
   c And she's wearing a uniform and some glasses. ☐
3 a She's standing near the teacher's desk. ☐
   b In the class, there are no teachers. ☐
   c I think she's waiting for the teacher. ☐

11 Discuss the questions in pairs.
1 What are your favorite colors?   3 Which do you not like?
2 How do they make you feel?   4 How do they make you feel?

Personal Best   Describe the colors in the rooms in your house or apartment and say how they make you feel.

9 LANGUAGE
how often + expressions of frequency ■ shopping

9C Love it or hate it?

1 Complete phrases 1–5 with the words in the box.

buy   pay   shop   sell   try on

1 _____ shoes
2 _____ by credit card
3 _____ fruit
4 _____ online
5 _____ a car

Go to Vocabulary practice: shopping, page 130

2 Do the questionnaire in pairs. Write down your partner's answers. Then go to page 147 and look at the results.

Shopping – do you love it or hate it?

1 How often do you go to a shopping mall?
a   Never! I hate malls.
b   I only go when I need some new clothes.
c   I go there every week. I love it!

2 Do you spend a lot of money on clothes and shoes?
a   No, I don't. I usually buy used clothes.
b   When I have a special occasion – once or twice a year.
c   Yes, I do. Clothes are very important to me.

3 How often do you shop online?
a   Not often. Maybe once a year.
b   A few times a month.
c   Very often. Three or four times a week.

4 How do you feel if you need to buy a present for someone?
a   Bored. I prefer to give cash as a present.
b   Happy. I can find something in a local store.
c   Really excited! I can go shopping all day on Saturday!

5 How do you usually pay when you go shopping?
a   I pay with cash. I never spend money that I don't have.
b   I sometimes pay with cash and sometimes by card.
c   I usually pay by credit card.

3 A Complete the questions and sentences from the questionnaire with the words in the box.

how   every   times   twice   often   once

1 How _____ do you go to a shopping mall?
2 I go there _____ week.
3 Once or _____ a year.
4 _____ often do you shop online?
5 Maybe _____ a year.
6 Three or four _____ a week.

B Which tense do we use to talk about the frequency of events? *simple present / present continuous*
Read the Grammar box.

how often + expressions of frequency ■ shopping **LANGUAGE 9C**

📖 **Grammar** *how often* + expressions of frequency

How often do you go shopping?

| I go shopping | once a
twice a
three/four times a
every | day/week/month/year |

Go to Grammar practice: *how often* + expressions of frequency, page 104

4 A ▶9.14 **Pronunciation:** sentence stress Listen and repeat the expressions of frequency. Pay attention to the underlined stressed words.

1 <u>once</u> a <u>day</u>
2 <u>twice</u> a <u>year</u>
3 <u>three</u> <u>times</u> a <u>month</u>
4 <u>every</u> <u>day</u> and <u>every</u> <u>night</u>

B ▶9.15 Say the sentences. Pay attention to the sentence stress. Listen, check and repeat.

1 I call my girlfriend twice a day.
2 We go to the movies every month.
3 They shop online three times a week.
4 My grandparents visit every year.

Go to Communication practice: Student A page 141, Student B page 149

5 A Write the questions.

1 How often / you buy someone a present?
_____
_____
_____

4 How often / it snow in your town?
_____
_____
_____

2 How often / your teacher give homework?
_____
_____
_____

5 How often / you go to bed after midnight?
_____
_____
_____

3 How often / you wash your hair?
_____
_____
_____

6 How often / you pay by credit card?
_____
_____
_____

B In pairs, ask and answer the questions.

A *How often do you buy someone a present?*
B *I buy someone a present once or twice a month. How about you?*

6 A Write three true sentences and three false sentences about you with expressions of frequency.
B Read your sentences to your partner. Guess if they are true or false.

A *I go to Singapore twice a year.*
B *I think that's false.*
A *No, it's true! My sister lives there.*

Personal Best Write some more questions about shopping for a questionnaire.

83

9 SKILLS WRITING describing a photo ■ describing position

9D Garage sale

1 A What do you do with things you don't use any more?

a Throw them away.
b Take them to a thrift store.
c Sell them online.
d Have a garage sale.

B Discuss the questions in pairs.

1 How often do you buy used things?
2 What type of used things do you buy?
3 Do people have garage sales in your country?
4 Do you think they're a good idea? Why/Why not?

2 A Read the e-mail quickly. What relationship is the writer to Patrick?

B Read the e-mail again. Match the names in the box with the people in the picture.

Bill   Sandra   Evie   Eddie

Hi Patrick,

How are you?

a We had a garage sale yesterday. It was at our house, and we sold some old clothes, books and other things.

b Here's a photo. The man on the right is our friend, Bill. He's looking at our old things. His wife Sandra is on the left, and the girl in the middle is their daughter, Evie. She's trying on my old hat. There's an old skateboard at the bottom of the photo – I think it's your dad's. The man at the top of the picture is our neighbor, Eddie. He's looking at a pair of Grandpa's old pants!

c We made about $100! We bought some new chairs for the yard with the money.

E-mail me soon with your news.

Grandma

3 A Match paragraphs a–c with the parts of the e-mail 1–3.

1 description of photo _____
2 what happened after _____
3 introduction _____

B What tenses are the verbs in paragraphs a–c? Read the Skill box.

Skill describing a photo

When we describe a photo, we:
- explain who the people are: *The man on the right is our friend, Bill.*
- use the present continuous to say what they are doing: *She's trying on my old hat.*
- use *there is/are* to say what things are in the picture: *There's an old skateboard …*

describing a photo ▪ describing position **WRITING** **SKILLS** **9D**

4 Complete Patrick's reply with the correct form of the verbs in parentheses.

Dear Grandma,

I'm very well, thanks. That's great about the garage sale!

I ¹_____ (go) to Bristol last Saturday with some friends. We ²_____ (take) the train in the morning, and we ³_____ (explore) the city.

Here's a photo. The girl on the left is Sara, and the girl in the middle is Lisa. They ⁴_____ (be) my classmates from college. They ⁵_____ (try) to find the Clifton Suspension Bridge on the map. Lisa's boyfriend, Shaun, is on the right. He ⁶_____ (take) a photo of some street art.

It was a fun day out, but we ⁷_____ (be) all really tired when we ⁸_____ (get) home!

Love Patrick x

5 Match the halves to make sentences. Check your answers in the e-mails.

1 The man on
2 The girl in
3 There's an old skateboard at
4 The man at
5 The girl on

a the left is Sara.
b the middle is their daughter, Evie.
c the right is our friend, Bill.
d the top of the picture is our neighbor, Eddie.
e the bottom of the photo.

Text builder describing position

◆ on the right   ◆ at the top   ✕ in the middle
◆ on the left   ◆ at the bottom ◣ in the corner

6 A Read the Text builder. Then write sentences.

1 that / my brother / right   _That's my brother on the right._
2 my friend Casey / middle   _____
3 there / a cat / corner   _____
4 that / my cousin / top   _____
5 there / more people / left   _____

B In pairs, take a photo of some of your classmates. Describe the photo using phrases from the Text builder.

That's Nacho on the left, and Lola is on the right. There's a blue purse in the corner. It's Lola's purse.

7 A PREPARE Choose one of the photos. Imagine that you took it. Make notes to answer the questions.

1 When and where did you take the photo?
2 Who are the people in the photo?
3 What are they doing?
4 What happened after you took the photo?

B PRACTICE Write an e-mail. Introduce the photo, describe it, and say what happened after you took it.

C PERSONAL BEST Exchange e-mails with your partner and read his/her work. Check the tenses of the verbs and prepositions for describing position. Can you improve anything?

Personal Best Write an e-mail describing one of your own photos.

85

UNIT 10 Time out

LANGUAGE present continuous for future plans ■ free-time activities

10A What are you doing on the weekend?

1 A Look at the poster for a music festival. Discuss the questions in pairs.
1 Do you know this music festival?
2 Where and when is the festival?
3 Do you like music festivals? Why/Why not?
4 What can you see in the pictures?

B Complete the text with the words in the box.

visit   go   watch   have   stay

COACHELLA Music and Arts Festival

April 14–16
Coachella Valley, California

Win tickets for an incredible Coachella experience

  Call 08081 570000 and tell us why you want to go.

1 _____ to all the concerts
2 _____ in a luxury tent
3 _____ the art area and see amazing sculptures
4 _____ movies at night
5 _____ a good time!

 Go to Vocabulary practice: free-time activities, page 131

2 ▶10.2 Read and listen to the conversation between two friends. Where is Alex going this weekend?

Alex Guess what I'm doing this weekend.
Dan I don't know. Are you visiting your family again?
Alex No, I'm not. I'm going to a music festival – Coachella! I won tickets in a contest.
Dan Coachella? No way! Which bands are playing?
Alex Radiohead is playing on Friday, and Lady Gaga on Saturday.
Dan That's awesome. Are you going on your own?
Alex No, the prize was two tickets.
Dan Two tickets? You know, I'm not doing anything this weekend ...
Alex I'm sorry, Dan. I'm going with my mom.
Dan Your mom?
Alex Yeah, she loves Lady Gaga. We're driving there tonight and then we're staying in a tent all weekend!
Dan Well, have a good time. Tell me all about it on Monday, OK?

3 Are the sentences true (T) or false (F)? Check your answers in the conversation.
1 Dan's going to Coachella with Alex. ____
2 Lady Gaga's playing on Saturday. ____
3 They're driving to the festival tonight. ____
4 They're staying in a hotel all weekend. ____

present continuous for future plans ■ free-time activities   LANGUAGE 10A

4 A Look at the sentences in exercise 3 again. Answer the questions.
1 Which tense are the verbs? *simple present / simple past / present continuous*
2 When do the actions happen? *in the past / now / in the future*

B Find more examples of this tense in the conversation in exercise 2. Then read the Grammar box.

Grammar — present continuous for future plans

Affirmative:
I**'m going** to a music festival this weekend.
We**'re visiting** a museum tomorrow.

Negative:
She**'s not going** to the concert tonight.
They**'re not staying** in a hotel.

Questions and short answers:
Are you **having** a party in the summer?
Yes, I **am**.   No, I**'m not**.

Go to Grammar practice: present continuous for future plans, page 105

5 A ▶10.5 **Pronunciation: sentence stress** Listen and repeat the questions and answers from the conversation in exercise 2. Pay attention to the underlined stressed words.
1 Are you <u>visiting</u> your <u>family</u>?   <u>No</u>, I'm <u>not</u>.
2 <u>Which</u> <u>bands</u> are <u>playing</u>?   <u>Radiohead</u> is <u>playing</u> on <u>Friday</u>.

B ▶10.6 Match the questions with answers a–c. Ask and answer the questions in pairs with the correct stress. Listen, check and repeat.
1 What are you doing this weekend?   a I'm taking the bus.
2 How are you getting there?   b Yes, I am.
3 Are you staying with friends?   c I'm going to the beach.

6 Look at Rosie's diary on her smartphone. In pairs, ask and answer the question *What's she doing …?* with the times in the box.

~~this morning~~   on Friday   tomorrow   on the weekend
the day after tomorrow   this evening

A *What's she doing this morning?*
B *She's having coffee with Kate.*

Go to Communication practice:
Student A page 141, Student B page 149

7 A ▶10.7 Use the words to write questions in the present continuous. Listen to the conversation and check.
1 What / you / do / on the weekend?
_____
2 Who / you / go / with?
_____
3 How / you / get / there?
_____
4 When / you / leave?
_____
5 Where / you / stay?
_____

B ▶10.7 Listen again and write Cheryl's answers to the questions.

8 A Make notes about your plans for the weekend. They can be real or imaginary.
B In pairs, ask and answer the questions in exercise 7 about your plans.
A *What are you doing on the weekend?*   B *I'm having a barbecue with my friends.*

Personal Best   Write a paragraph about your "perfect" weekend.

87

10 SKILLS
READING scanning for information ■ the imperative ■ types of music and movies

10B What's on?

1 ▶ 10.8 Listen and match the words in the box with the types of music and movies.

> classical science fiction action jazz electronic romance

1 _____ 2 _____ 3 _____ 4 _____ 5 _____ 6 _____

Go to Vocabulary practice: types of music and movies, page 132

Personal Best

2 Look at the webpage on page 89. What type of website is it? Do you use websites like this?

🔧 Skill scanning for information

"Scanning" means looking quickly at a text to find specific information.
- <u>Underline</u> the key word(s) in the question.
- Look for the word(s) in the text quickly. Use your finger to help you.
- When you find the word, read the information to answer the question.

3 A Read the Skill box. Then read questions 1–4 and scan the text for the answers. The key words are <u>underlined</u>.

1 What time does the <u>concert</u> start? _____
2 Where is the art <u>exhibition</u>? _____
3 How much is a <u>movie</u> ticket for children? _____
4 Which event is <u>free</u> to enter? _____

B Read questions 1–4 and <u>underline</u> the key words. Then scan the text for the answers.

1 What's the name of the movie theater in the city? _____
2 How old do you need to be to try speed dating? _____
3 Which event costs less if you buy tickets online? _____
4 Who's playing electronic music tonight? _____

4 Look at the text and discuss the questions in pairs.

1 Which events do you want to go to? Why?
2 Which events are you not interested in? Why?

5 Complete the sentences from the text with the correct words.

1 Don't _____ it!
2 _____ to our Speed Dating night!
3 _____ all night.
4 _____ very scared!

🧩 Text builder the imperative

We use the imperative to give instructions.
Book *early!* ***Open*** *the window!* ***Don't be*** *late!* ***Don't forget*** *about the party!*

6 Read the Text builder. Then complete the sentences with the affirmative or negative imperative of the verbs in the box.

> call listen talk sit open be

1 _____ down, please. I can't see the movie.
2 The concert starts at 7:45, so _____ late.
3 _____ to this great song. I love it!
4 _____ the window, please. It's very hot.
5 Please _____ in the library. I'm trying to read.
6 _____ me today because I'm working.

7 Discuss the questions in pairs.

1 What's your favorite type of music?
2 When do you listen to music?
3 How often do you go to concerts/clubs?
4 What type of movies do you like?
5 What was the last movie you saw?
6 How often do you go to the movies?

scanning for information ■ the imperative ■ types of music and movies   READING   SKILLS   10B

What's On

Events in your area: Saturday, June 9   Sort by: Date

Visitors
Science-fiction adventure. When aliens arrive on Earth, do they want to help people – or start a war?
ABC Movie Theater, 6:30 p.m. 9:00 p.m. 11:30 p.m.
Tickets $10. Under 16: $8

Buy Tickets

Anderson .Paak in concert
Anderson .Paak brings his mix of jazz, hip-hop, and rock to the city. Don't miss it!
Royal Arena, 8:00 p.m.
Tickets $17.50

Sold Out

Romeo and Juliet
William Shakespeare's great love story. A boy and a girl find love on the streets of Verona.
King's Theater, 7:15 p.m.
Tickets $18.00

Sold Out

Underwater garden
Dance all night as DJ Octopus plays the latest in electronic music from around the world.
Club Infinity, 10:00 p.m.–late   Admission $8.00 (Over 18 only)

Buy Tickets

Hot Potato
Enjoy an evening of comedy with Sally Quentin. "Really funny" *The Daily Times*. Book online and save $5.
Comedy Club, 7:00 p.m.
Tickets $15 at the door

Buy Tickets

Looking for love?
Are you single? Do you want to find that special person? Come to our Speed Dating night – the fun way to meet new people!
Union Coffee Shop, 6:30 p.m.
Admission $15. Minimum age 21

Buy Tickets

Book reading with Joe Arnott
Joe Arnott reads from his new horror story, *Play With Fire*. Be scared, be very scared!
Forest Hill Library, 8:00 p.m.
Admission free. Over 16 only

Reserve

Picasso's portraits
Exhibition of paintings and sculptures by one of the most popular artists of the twentieth century.
Trinidad Gallery
Tickets $12.50

Buy Tickets

Personal Best Write information about three events in your town or city. Use imperatives.

10 LANGUAGE question review ■ sports and games

10C Royal hobbies

1 Complete the sports and games with the verbs *go*, *play* and *do*.

1 _____ tennis   2 _____ karate   3 _____ running   4 _____ rock climbing   5 _____ video games   6 _____ yoga

Go to Vocabulary practice: sports and games, page 133

2 In pairs, ask and answer the question *Do you ...?* with the correct verbs and the sports and games in the box.

A *Do you go bike riding?*   B *Yes, I do. I usually go bike riding once a week.*

bike riding   swimming   soccer   pilates   gymnastics   basketball   chess   karate   skiing

3 A Who are the people in the picture? Read the text and check. What do you know about them?

B ▶ 10.11 Guess which three activities in exercise 1 the people do. Listen to the interview and check.

4 A ▶ 10.11 Complete the interviewer's questions with the words in the box. Listen again and check.

was   where   how   does   is   what

1 _____ does he relax?
2 _____ is his favorite game?
3 _____ did she go to college?
4 _____ she good at sports?
5 _____ William exercise a lot too?
6 _____ he training for a marathon now?

B Look at questions 1–6 again.

1 Which questions do you answer with *yes* or *no*? ____ ____ ____
2 Which questions do you answer with specific information? ____ ____ ____

7:00 pm
Relaxing with the Royals

What do Prince Harry, Prince William and his wife Kate, the Duchess of Cambridge, do in their free time? Royal expert Jenny Brown joins us to talk about how the young royals relax.

5 A Match the tenses in the box with the questions in 4A.

simple past   present continuous   simple present (x2)   simple present of *be*   simple past of *be*

1 _____   2 _____   3 _____   4 _____   5 _____   6 _____

B Match the words in the box with the parts of the question 1–4. Then read the Grammar box.

subject   question word   main verb   auxiliary verb

1 What _____   2 do _____   3 they _____   4 do _____ in their free time?

question review ■ sports and games   LANGUAGE **10C**

 Grammar question review

Most verbs: (question word) + auxiliary verb + subject + main verb:
Where do you live?   What are you doing?   When did they arrive?
Does Carla play tennis?   Is he watching TV?   Did you go running yesterday?

The verb *be*: (question word) + *be* + subject:
How old are you?   Where was Antonio yesterday?
Is the milk in the refrigerator?   Were you worried about the exam?

Go to Grammar practice: question review, page 105

6 A ▶ 10.14 **Pronunciation:** Intonation in questions Listen and repeat the questions. Pay attention to the intonation that goes up (↗) or down (↘).

questions with question words   yes/ no questions
1 Which movies do you like? ↘   3 Is she from Japan? ↗
2 Where are they going? ↘   4 Did you stay in a hotel? ↗

B ▶ 10.15 Say the questions with the correct intonation. Listen, check and repeat. Then ask and answer the questions in pairs.

1 What are you doing tonight?   4 How often do you take the bus?
2 Did you cook dinner yesterday?   5 Is it raining right now?
3 Where were you at 7:00 this morning?   6 Does our teacher like pop music?

Go to Communication practice: Student A page 141, Student B page 150

7 A ▶ 10.16 Order the words to make questions 1–6. Listen and check.
B ▶ 10.16 In pairs, ask and answer the questions. Listen again and check.

Estonian fashion model Carmen Kass plays chess.	**American singer Elvis Presley did karate.**	**American actor Lucy Liu goes rock climbing.**
1 start / did / when / she _____?	3 karate / at / was / good / he _____?	5 go / how / rock climbing / she / does / often _____?
2 she / how / did / learn _____?	4 where / do / did / it / he _____?	6 dangerous / is / it _____?

8 Choose a sport or game that you play. In pairs, ask and answer the questions in the boxes.

- What sport or game do you play?
- When did you start?
- Where do you play it?
- How often do you play it?
- Are you playing it this weekend?
- Is it difficult?
- Is it expensive?
- How did you learn?
- Who do you play it with?
- What do you need to play it?

Personal Best Write a paragraph about a sport or game you enjoy.

91

10 **SKILLS** **SPEAKING** showing interest ■ asking about a tourist attraction

10D Where are we going now?

1 Look at the pictures and answer the questions.

1 Which tourist attractions can you see?
2 Which countries are they in?
3 Do you want to visit them? Why/Why not?
4 What tourist attractions are there in your town/city?

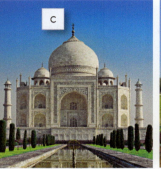

2 A ▶ 10.17 Watch or listen to the first part of *Learning Curve*. Where is Ethan? Who does he meet?

B ▶ 10.17 Choose the correct options to complete the sentences. Watch or listen again and check.

1 Flushing Meadows is famous for its *soccer stadium / tennis stadium*.
2 There were two World's Fairs in the park – in 1939 and in *1964 / 1974*.
3 There is a *science museum / design museum* in the park.
4 Ethan, Penny, and Taylor are meeting Marc in *half an hour / an hour*.
5 Marc and Taylor *know / don't know* each other.

3 ▶ 10.18 Listen and complete the questions in the conversation.

> **Taylor** So what time ¹_____ the Hall of Science _____?
> **Ethan** It opens at 10:00 am.
> **Penny** What ²_____ _____ to do if it rains?
> **Ethan** Well, we can stay inside and look at exhibits all day.
> **Penny** OK. Sounds good. When ³_____ it _____?
> **Ethan** 6:00 pm.
> **Taylor** OK, great. So, what ⁴_____ we _____ now?
> **Ethan** We're meeting our friend Marc from *Learning Curve*, at the Information Desk.

Conversation builder	asking about a tourist attraction
What time does it open/close?	*Is there a café/restaurant/gift shop?*
Which days is it open?	*What is there to do if it rains?*
How do you get there?	*Are there any special events?*

4 A Read the Conversation builder. Then look at the information about a tourist attraction on page 93. Ask and answer questions in pairs.

A *What time does it open?* **B** *It opens at 9:30 a.m.*

B Do you want to visit this attraction? Why/Why not?

showing interest ■ asking about a tourist attraction   **SPEAKING**   SKILLS   **10D**

Fun days out Legoland > Plan your trip   Week: September 13–19

| Monday | Tuesday | Wednesday | Thursday | Friday | Saturday | Sunday |

● 9:30 a.m. – 5:00 p.m. ($30)   ● 9:30 a.m. – 6:00 p.m. ($35)   ● Closed

Weather: Most attractions are outside. Umbrellas are available from the gift shop. Inside attractions include: Wells Fargo Fun Town 4D Theater, Imagination Zone and Pirates' Cove.

Food & drink: Fun Town Pizza & Pasta, Castle Burger and many more.

Getting there:
By car: Legoland is on International Drive (parking available).
By bus: Take the shuttle bus from the Orlando Eye.

December 31: Kids' New Year's Eve fireworks show

5 A ▶ 10.19 Watch or listen to the second part of the show. How many exhibits do Penny, Marc, Ethan, and Taylor see in the Hall of Science?

B ▶ 10.19 Are the sentences true (T) or false (F)? Watch or listen again and check.

1 Tickets for the Hall of Science cost $15. ____
2 There are almost 450 exhibits. ____
3 Marc and Ethan buy tickets for a 3D movie. ____
4 Taylor doesn't like flying. ____
5 Taylor wants a flying car. ____
6 They decide to eat pizza. ____

Penny   Ethan   Marc   Taylor

6 ▶ 10.20 Match the sentences with the responses. Listen, check and repeat the responses.

1 It costs $15, but we paid for you.
2 What about *Journey into Space*? It's a 3D movie.
3 We're hungry, and we're eating a very large pizza.

a OK. Sounds good.
b Oh really? Thanks!
c That sounds interesting!

🔧 **Skill**   showing interest

When people speak to you, it's important to show that you're listening.
• Use expressions: *Oh really? That sounds good. Great.*
• Use intonation to sound interested.

7 A ▶ 10.21 Read the Skill box. Then listen to conversations 1–4. Which response sounds more interested: *a* or *b*?

1 I'm visiting my family this weekend. ____
2 My sister goes rock climbing every week. ____
3 There's a new comedy at the movie theater. ____
4 We went to the beach yesterday. ____

B ▶ 10.22 Listen and repeat the interested responses.

Go to Communication practice: Students A and B, page 150

8 A PREPARE In pairs, invent a tourist attraction and write information about it. Include:

• the days and times it is open
• the price of tickets
• what you can do
• how to get there
• stores and restaurants
• special events

B PRACTICE Exchange your information with another pair. Then ask and answer questions about the tourist attraction. Remember to show you're interested.

A *What time does the museum open?*   B *It opens at 9:30 a.m.*   A *OK, great.*

C PERSONAL BEST Listen to the other pair. Do they ask questions well? Do they show interest?

Personal Best   Write about a tourist attraction in your town/city.

9 and 10 REVIEW and PRACTICE

Grammar

1 Check (✔) the correct sentences.

1 a I can't talk now. I'm doing my homework. ☐
  b I can't talk now. I do my homework. ☐
  c I can't talk now. I did my homework. ☐

2 a They not working right now. ☐
  b They're not working right now. ☐
  c They don't working right now. ☐

3 a What often do you go to the gym? ☐
  b How often do you go to the gym? ☐
  c How much often do you go to the gym? ☐

4 a I see my brother three times at year. ☐
  b I see my brother three times for year. ☐
  c I see my brother three times a year. ☐

5 a What are you doing tomorrow? ☐
  b What do you do tomorrow? ☐
  c What you are doing tomorrow? ☐

6 a He not is coming to the party tonight. ☐
  b He's not coming to the party tonight. ☐
  c He doesn't come to the party tonight. ☐

7 a What time did the train leave? ☐
  b What time the train did leave? ☐
  c What time left the train? ☐

8 a They were at work yesterday? ☐
  b Did they be at work yesterday? ☐
  c Were they at work yesterday? ☐

2 Complete the questions and sentences with the correct form of the verbs in the box.

> cost finish spend go take meet
> not be not study can buy wear

1 How often _____ you _____ a shower?
2 Carlos _____ some new boots today. Look – they're really nice.
3 What time _____ you _____ work last night?
4 We _____ shopping in New York next Tuesday.
5 How much _____ your new coat _____ ? Was it expensive?
6 She's in the library, but she _____ . She's texting a friend.
7 _____ you _____ your friends next weekend?
8 He _____ at work yesterday. I think he was sick.
9 Where _____ I _____ some good shoes?
10 How much money _____ you _____ on clothes every month?

3 Complete the text with the correct form of the verbs in parentheses.

The Kinderkook Café

The Kinderkook Café in Amsterdam is a café with a difference – the chefs and waiters are all children! Parents take their children to the café in the afternoon and the children cook a meal. Then, in the evening, the parents return to eat it. Matt Baker talked to one of the parents, Sonja Kroes.

Matt When ¹_____ the café _____ (start)?
Sonja It started in 1981. It's very popular.
Matt What ²_____ the children _____ (cook)?
Sonja They cook pasta, curry, pizza, and lots more. The food is healthy and delicious.
Matt How often ³_____ you _____ (come) here with your daughter?
Sonja We come once a month. Lotte loves it!
Matt ⁴_____ she _____ (work) here today?
Sonja Yes, she is. She ⁵_____ (bake) a cake. Look, she's over there. She ⁶_____ (wear) a pink sweater. And her friend, Stijn, is helping her. They ⁷_____ (have) a good time!
Matt ⁸_____ you _____ (eat) here tonight?
Sonja Yes, I am. I ⁹_____ (come) with my husband and my parents. It was Lotte's birthday yesterday, and she wanted to have a small party here with the family.
Matt That's nice. How old ¹⁰_____ (be) she?
Sonja She's seven.

Vocabulary

1 Put the words in the box in the correct columns.

> volleyball a museum videogames a suit yoga
> an art gallery shopping bike riding gymnastics
> karate pants walking tennis my family a belt

go	do	visit	wear	play

94

REVIEW and PRACTICE 9 and 10

2 Circle the word that is different. Explain your answers.
1 angry   happy   hockey   thirsty
2 skirt   beach   jacket   dress
3 festival concert   suit   party
4 tent   pay   spend   buy
5 pop   rock   jazz   coat
6 socks   boots   shoes   pants
7 museum   art gallery sweater department store
8 money   comedy   romance   drama

3 Choose the correct options to complete the sentences.
1 Can I try _____ this shirt, please?
   a in   b off   c on
2 That store _____ really nice T-shirts.
   a sells   b spends   c pays
3 Let's have dinner _____ home tonight.
   a in   b at   c on
4 Do you want to _____ a movie?
   a go   b look   c watch
5 I don't have any money. Can I pay _____ card?
   a with   b by   c for
6 I usually shop _____ . I don't have time to go to the grocery store.
   a online   b by card   c by cash
7 We're _____ a barbecue this weekend. Would you like to come?
   a having   b staying   c spending
8 We don't accept credit cards here. Can you pay with _____ , please?
   a chess   b cash   c calm

4 Complete the conversation with the words in the box.

| hungry | excited | time | scared |
| horror | bored | happy | tired |

Bella What did you do last night, Ruby?
Ruby Tim and I went to the movie theater. We watched that new ¹_____ movie, *Black Night*.
Bella Were you ²_____ ?
Ruby No, we were ³_____ . It wasn't very good.
Bella That's too bad. Did you do anything after the movie?
Ruby We were really ⁴_____ , so we went to a restaurant.
Bella How was the food?
Ruby It was excellent, so we were ⁵_____ ! What about you? What did you do?
Bella We went to a concert – the Foo Fighters. They're Nick's favorite band. He was very ⁶_____ when he got tickets.
Ruby Did you have a good ⁷_____ ?
Bella Yes, it was great. The concert finished at 1:00 in the morning, so I'm really ⁸_____ today!

95

GRAMMAR PRACTICE

6A there is/are

We use *there's* (*there is*) + *a/an* with singular nouns to say that something exists.
There's a beautiful park near my house.   *There's an umbrella on the table.*
We use *there are* with plural nouns to say that something exists.
There are five hotels in my city.   *There are six people on the bus.*
We often use *some* in affirmative sentences with plural nouns. We use *any* in negative sentences and questions with plural nouns.
There are some good stores downtown.   *There aren't any museums.*
Are there any hotels near here?
We can also make negative sentences with *no*:
There's no museum.   *There are no museums.*

▶ 6.2	Singular	Plural
+	There's a school. There's an airport.	There are some schools. There are two airports.
−	There's no theater.	There aren't any / There are no theaters.
?	Is there a restaurant?	Are there any restaurants?
Y/N	Yes, there is. / No, there isn't. No, there's not.	Yes, there are. / No, there aren't.

1 Complete the sentences with the correct forms of *there is/are*.
  1 _____ a great museum in town.
  2 _____ a school near your house?
  3 I'm sorry, but _____ no drugstore near here.
  4 _____ some cheap hotels near the train station.
  5 _____ any parks, so children play in the street.
  6 _____ any good restaurants at the shopping mall?

2 Complete the sentences with *a/an*, *some* or *any*.
  1 There aren't _____ supermarkets in this area.
  2 There's _____ good hospital near here.
  3 There are _____ police officers in the street.
  4 There isn't _____ Italian restaurant in our town.
  5 Are there _____ pens in your purse?
  6 Is there _____ police station near here?

◀ Go back to page 51

6C Prepositions of place

We use prepositions of place to say where an object or person is.
There's a table next to the bed.   *Your keys are behind the sofa.*
My brother is in the kitchen.   *Simon is next to Amy.*

▶ 6.9   Prepositions of place

on	 The phone is **on** the table.	next to	 The chair is **next to** the table.
in	 The phone is **in** the purse.	in front of	 The table is **in front of** the chair.
above	 The shelves are **above** the table.	between	 The chair is **between** the window and the table.
under	The purse is **under** the table.	behind	 The lamp is **behind** the sofa.

1 Look at the picture. Write sentences saying where the things are with prepositions of place.
  1 refrigerator / stove
  _____
  2 shelves / bed
  _____
  3 cat / table
  _____
  4 laptop / desk
  _____
  5 window / sofa
  _____
  6 table / sofa
  _____

◀ Go back to page 55

GRAMMAR PRACTICE

7A Simple past: *be*

We use the simple past of the verb *be* to talk about situations in the past.

Marilyn Monroe was an actor. She was American.

The affirmative simple past forms of the verb *be* are *was* and *were*.

I was in New York yesterday. The people were very friendly.

The negative simple past forms of the verb *be* are *wasn't* (*was not*) and *weren't* (*were not*).

I wasn't at home last night.
The Beatles weren't from Manchester.

We form questions with *was/were* + subject.

Was the teacher late for class?
Were you cold at work today?

▶ 7.2	I / he / she / it	you / we / they
+	I **was** happy.	They **were** singers.
–	It **wasn't** a good movie.	We **weren't** at home yesterday.
?	**Was** she at school?	**Were** they Mexican?
Y/N	Yes, she **was**. / No, she **wasn't**.	Yes, they **were**. / No, they **weren't**.

1 Choose the correct words to complete the sentences.
 1 My father *was* / *were* an artist.
 2 Enrique and Javier *wasn't* / *weren't* at work on Monday.
 3 How *was* / *were* your vacation?
 4 This book *wasn't* / *weren't* very interesting.
 5 My grandparents *was* / *were* both musicians.
 6 What *was* / *were* the answer to this question?
 7 *Were* / *Was* you and your sister at home yesterday?
 8 We *wasn't* / *weren't* happy with our grades.

2 Complete the conversations with the correct form of *was* or *were*.
 1 A _____ you at home yesterday?
  B No, I _____ . I _____ at the hospital.
 2 A _____ the movie good?
  B Yes, it _____ . The actors _____ amazing.
 3 A _____ your parents teachers?
  B No, they _____ . They _____ writers.
 4 A _____ Akira Kurosawa a photographer?
  B No, he _____ . He _____ a movie director.
 5 A _____ you late for school today?
  B Yes, I _____ . I _____ 30 minutes late.
 6 A _____ you and Nico at the same school?
  B Yes, we _____ , but we _____ in the same class.

◀ Go back to page 61

7C Simple past: regular verbs

We use the simple past to talk about completed actions in the past. We usually add *-ed* to the base form to form the simple past of regular verbs.

cook ⇨ cooked   *I cooked pasta yesterday.*

Spelling rules for regular affirmative simple past verbs

We usually add *-ed* to the base form.
cook ⇨ cooked

When a verb ends in *-e*, we add *-d*.
dance ⇨ danced

When a verb ends in consonant + *y*, we change the *y* to *i* and then we add *-ed*.
study ⇨ studied

When a verb ends in vowel + consonant, we usually double the consonant and add *-ed*.
stop ⇨ stopped

We form the negative with *didn't* (*did not*) + base form.

I didn't want coffee for breakfast.   *My parents didn't like the food.*

We form questions with *did* + subject + base form.

Did she play the piano yesterday?   *Did your brother live in Canada?*

▶ 7.12	I / you / he / she / it / we / they
+	He **worked** in Washington.
–	They **didn't live** in this house.
?	**Did** you **study** Spanish in college?
Y/N	Yes, I **did**. / No, I **didn't**.

1 Rewrite the sentences and questions in the simple past.

 1 My grandfather lives on this street.
  _____
 2 I cook paella for lunch.
  _____
 3 She doesn't ride her bike home.
  _____
 4 The train doesn't stop in Paris.
  _____
 5 Liam studies science in college.
  _____
 6 Does she dance with her friends?
  _____
 7 Do they live in Ecuador?
  _____
 8 Elise doesn't want ice cream.
  _____

◀ Go back to page 65

GRAMMAR PRACTICE

8A Simple past: irregular verbs

A lot of common verbs have an irregular simple past form (for a full list of irregular verbs see page 151).

take ⇨ took   I took a taxi to the airport.
go ⇨ went   We went to the park yesterday.
buy ⇨ bought I bought a new purse.

Only the affirmative forms are irregular. We form the negative with *didn't* + base form.

We didn't take the train.
They didn't go to the party.
My sister didn't buy coffee.

We form questions with *did* + subject + base form.

Did they take the train?
Did you go to the grocery store?
Did we buy any vegetables?

▶ 8.2	I / you / he / she / it / we / they
+	He **went** to college in Boston.
–	She **didn't have** breakfast yesterday.
?	**Did** you **see** Carly at the party?
Y/N	Yes, I **did**. / No, I **didn't**.

1 Complete the sentences with the simple past form of the verbs in parentheses.

1 They _____ to work by car. (go)
2 She _____ to Hong Kong. (fly)
3 I _____ on the 11:30 bus to Newcastle. (get)
4 Paula _____ her daughter a lot of stories. (tell)
5 Richard _____ coffee and toast for breakfast. (have)
6 Clarissa _____ "Hi". (say)
7 I _____ pasta for dinner. (make)
8 My mom _____ to work yesterday. (drive)

2 Complete the questions and answers with the correct form of the verbs in parentheses.

1 A What time _____ her train _____ ? (leave)
  B It _____ at 8:00 p.m.
2 A _____ you _____ a dress to the party? (wear)
  B No, I _____ a dress. I _____ jeans.
3 A _____ he _____ a bus to the station? (take)
  B No, he _____ a bus. He _____ the subway.
4 A _____ you _____ well last night? (sleep)
  B No, I _____ at all!
5 A _____ you _____ a big lunch? (have)
  B No, I _____. I _____ a sandwich.
6 A _____ you _____ to your dad yesterday? (speak)
  B No, but I _____ to my mom.

◀ Go back to page 69

8C there was/were

We use *there was* and *a/an* with singular nouns to say that something existed in the past.

There was a big school here 50 years ago.
There was an egg in the refrigerator yesterday.

We use *there were* with plural nouns to say that something existed in the past.

There were lots of fields here in the past.
There were two books on my desk.

We often use *some* in affirmative sentences with plural nouns. We use *any* in negative sentences and questions. We can also use *no* with a singular or plural noun after *there was/were*.

There were some people in the store.
There weren't any children. / There were no children.
Were there any cakes in the grocery store?

▶ 8.9	Singular	Plural
+	**There was** a road. **There was** an old house.	**There were** two stores. **There were some** trees.
–	**There was no** library. / **There wasn't** a library.	**There were no** restaurants. / **There weren't any** restaurants.
?	**Was there** a school?	**Were there any** tall buildings?
Y/N	Yes, **there was**. / No, **there wasn't**.	Yes, **there were**. / No, **there weren't**.

1 Look at the picture of Fairfield 100 years ago. Complete the sentences with the correct form of *there was/were* and *a/an* or *some/any/no*.

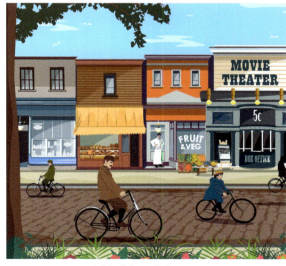

1 _____ tall buildings, but _____ stores.
2 _____ cars in the town, but _____ bicycles.
3 _____ movie theater, but _____ club.
4 _____ old tree and _____ flowers.

◀ Go back to page 73

103

GRAMMAR PRACTICE

9A Present continuous

We use the present continuous to talk about actions that are happening now. We often use time expressions like *right now* and *at the moment* with the present continuous.

I'm wearing my new jeans today.
We're not working at the moment.
What are you doing now?

We form the present continuous with the verb *be* + the *-ing* form of the main verb.

Spelling rules for the *-ing* form

We usually add *-ing* to the base form of the verb.
cook ⇨ cooking   watch ⇨ watching

When the verb ends in a consonant + *e*, we usually remove the *e* and then add *-ing*.
take ⇨ taking   dance ⇨ dancing

When the verb ends in a consonant + a vowel + a consonant, we double the consonant and then add *-ing*.
begin ⇨ beginning   get ⇨ getting

▶ 9.3	I	he / she / it	you / we / they
+	I'm listening to music.	He's reading a book.	You're singing.
−	I'm not watching TV.	She's not working.	We're not stopping here.
?	Am I sleeping?	Is he studying?	Are they going?
Y/N	Yes, I am. / No, I'm not.	Yes, he is. / No, he's not. / No, he isn't.	Yes, they are. / No, they're not.

1 Write the *-ing* form of the verbs.
  1 buy _____   6 look _____
  2 drive _____   7 make _____
  3 sit _____   8 stop _____
  4 go _____   9 swim _____
  5 leave _____   10 watch _____

2 Write affirmative (+) sentences, negative (−) sentences or questions (?) in the present continuous.
  1 George / listen to / music / now (+)
  _____
  2 you / wear / a new coat (?)
  _____
  3 she / listen to / me (−)
  _____
  4 they / do / their homework (−)
  _____
  5 we / have dinner / at the moment (+)
  _____
  6 it / rain / today (?)
  _____

◀ Go back to page 79

9C How often + expressions of frequency

We use *How often ...?* + the simple present or the verb *be* to ask about frequency.

How often do you go shopping?
How often does Tim go to London?
How often are you late for class?

We can answer the question *How often ...?* with expressions of frequency.

How often are your English classes?
I have a class once or twice a week. (*once* = one time, *twice* = two times)

▶ 9.13	Expressions of frequency
every day/week/month/year	I go to the gym **every day**.
once a day/week/month/year	John has a vacation **once a year**.
twice a day/week/month/year	Ali has a coffee with his friends **twice a week**.
three/four times a day/week/month/year	They play soccer **three or four times a month**.

Look! We can also answer questions with *How often ...?* with frequency adverbs (*always, usually, often, sometimes, never*).
How often do you walk to work?
I never walk to work. I usually get the bus.

1 Complete the questions and answers. Use the words in parentheses.

  1 How often _____ your bike? (you / ride)
    I _____ my bike _____ day.
  2 How often _____ in your city? (it / snow)
    It only _____ once _____ year.
  3 How often _____ his grandparents? (Luis / see)
    He _____ his grandparents three _____ a month.
  4 How often _____ tennis? (you / play)
    We _____ tennis _____ weekend.
  5 How often _____ their friends? (they / meet)
    They _____ their friends twice _____ week.

◀ Go back to page 83

GRAMMAR PRACTICE

10A Present continuous for future plans

We use the present continuous to talk about plans and arrangements in the future (for spelling rules of -ing forms see page 104).

I'm going to the dentist next week.

▶ 10.3	I	he / she / it	you / we / they
+	I'm meeting friends tonight.	She's taking the bus tomorrow.	You're working next Tuesday.
−	I'm not going to school tomorrow.	He's not watching a movie tonight.	We're not playing tennis later.
?	Am I working this weekend?	Is she staying home tonight?	Are they going to the gym?
Y/N	Yes, I am. / No, I'm not.	Yes, she is. / No, she's not.	Yes, they are. / No, they're not.

We often use a future time expression to talk about future plans and arrangements. Time expressions usually go at the end of the sentence.

▶ 10.4	Future time expressions
this morning/afternoon/evening	We're taking the train **this afternoon**.
tonight	What are you having for dinner **tonight**?
tomorrow	Sven isn't coming to the party **tomorrow**.
next week/month/year	We're going on vacation **next week**.
later	Are you meeting Jorge **later**?

10C Question review

Questions can be *yes/no* questions or they can ask for specific information with a question word (*where, when, who*, etc.).

Do you live in Japan? Yes, I do. / No, I don't.
Where are you from?   I'm from Turkey.

For most verbs, the word order in questions is: (question word +) auxiliary verb + subject + base form of main verb + rest of question.

▶ 10.12	(Question word)	Auxiliary verb	Subject	Main verb	Rest of question
Simple present		Does	Chris	speak	English?
	What	do	you	have	for breakfast?
Simple past		Did	Lucy	call	you yesterday?
	When	did	you	arrive	at the airport?
Present continuous		Is	it	snowing	now?
	Where	are	they	going	next week?

For the verbs *be* and *can*, the word order in questions is: (question word +) verb + subject + rest of question.

▶ 10.13	(Question word)	Verb	Subject	Rest of question
be (simple present)		Is	Julia	here?
	Where	are	you	from?
be (simple past)		Were	you	late for work?
	Who	was	Philip	with?
can		Can	you	ride a motorcycle?
	What sports	can	they	play?

1 Complete the sentences and questions with the present continuous form of the verbs in the box.

> take   not visit   meet
> not come   stay   watch

1 We _____ our friends for dinner later.
2 _____ you _____ the soccer game tonight?
3 They _____ the 7:30 train to Edinburgh tomorrow.
4 He _____ with some friends in Lima at the weekend.
5 Maria is sick. She _____ to the concert this evening.
6 We _____ the museum next week. It's closed.

2 Write sentences and questions in the present continuous.

1 I / meet / my friends this weekend
_____.
2 My brother / not visit / us this month
_____.
3 They / not go / on vacation this summer
_____.
4 What / you / cook / for dinner on Saturday
_____?

◀ Go back to page 87

1 Order the words to make questions.

1 rock climbing / does / go / how often / he
_____?
2 you / what / for / lunch / are / having
_____?
3 homework / when / she / did / do / her
_____?
4 can / instrument / you / play / an
_____?
5 you / crying / why / are
_____?
6 did / where / he / on / go / vacation
_____?
7 they / were / home / night / last / at
_____?
8 what / is / she / time / leaving
_____?

◀ Go back to page 91

105

VOCABULARY PRACTICE

6A Places in town

1 ▶ 6.1 Listen and repeat.

1 bank　　2 bus stop　　3 café　　4 club

5 hospital　　6 hotel　　7 movie theater　　8 museum

9 park　　10 police station　　11 post office　　12 restaurant

13 school　　14 shopping mall　　15 grocery store　　16 train station

Look!

A town is small or medium-sized.
A city is big.

a town　　*a city*

2 Match the places in the box with jobs 1–5.

| hospital   police station   school |
| restaurant   shopping mall |

1 waiter _____
2 police officer _____
3 salesclerk _____
4 teacher _____
5 doctor _____

3 Complete the sentences with the places in the box.

| bank   club   train station   park   post office   grocery store |
| bus stop   café   movie theater   museum |

1 You can send a letter at a _____ .
2 You can catch a train at a _____ .
3 You wait for a bus at a _____ .
4 You drink tea or coffee at a _____ .
5 You can dance at a _____ .
6 You watch a movie at a _____ .
7 You see interesting things at a _____ .
8 You get money at a _____ .
9 You walk, play games, or relax in a _____ .
10 You can buy food and drinks at a _____ .

◀ Go back to page 50

VOCABULARY PRACTICE

6B Parts of the body

1 ▶ 6.7 Listen and repeat.

Look! The plural of *tooth* is *teeth*. The plural of *foot* is *feet*.

2 Put the parts of the body in the box in the correct columns.

| arms body ears face feet hands head knees legs mouth nose teeth |

I have one …	I have two …	I have more than two …

◀ Go back to page 52

121

> **VOCABULARY PRACTICE**

6C Rooms and furniture

1 ▶ 6.8 Listen and repeat.

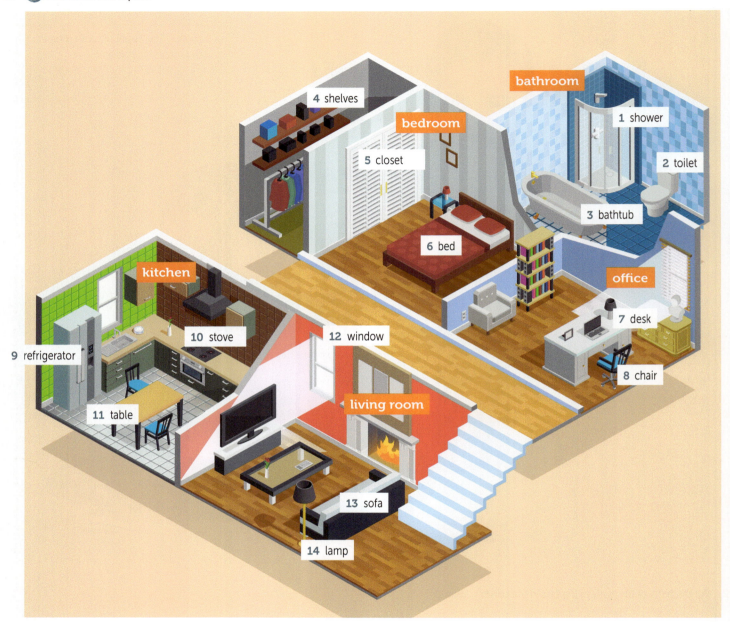

2 Complete the sentences with the rooms and furniture in the box.

| refrigerator | bathtub | table | sofa | desk | window | bedroom | stove | closet | shelves |

1 Let's have dinner in the living room. We can sit on the _____ and watch a movie.
2 Shona has a big walk-in _____ for all her clothes.
3 My favorite room is my _____ . I sleep there, and it's very quiet.
4 After we make dinner, the _____ is very hot.
5 My bathroom is small, so I take a shower, but I don't have a _____ .
6 Angie needs a lot of _____ because she has hundreds of books!
7 It's hot in here. Can you open the _____ ?
8 Please put the milk and orange juice in the _____ .
9 I have a _____ in my bedroom where I do homework and use my laptop.
10 Dinner's ready. The food's on the _____ !

◀ Go back to page 54

VOCABULARY PRACTICE

7A Celebrities

1 ▶ 7.1 Listen and repeat.

1 artist

2 athlete

3 dancer

4 DJ

5 fashion model

6 journalist

7 king

8 movie director

9 musician

10 photographer

11 politician

12 queen

13 racing driver

14 soccer player

15 tennis player

16 writer

2 Look at the pictures and complete the sentences with the words in the box.

| fashion model | writer | queen | musician | tennis player | dancer | king | movie director | artist | soccer player | politician | athlete |

1 Shelly-Ann Fraser-Pryce is a Jamaican _____.

2 Gisele Bündchen is a Brazilian _____.

3 Emmanuel Macron is a French _____.

4 Isabel Allende is a Chilean _____.

5 Thomas Müller is a German _____.

6 Margrethe II is the _____ of Denmark.

7 Salvador Dalí was a Spanish _____.

8 Beyoncé is an American _____.

9 Sofia Coppola is an American _____.

10 Venus Williams is an American _____.

11 Felipe VI is the _____ of Spain.

12 Rudolf Nureyev was a Russian _____.

◀ Go back to page 60

VOCABULARY PRACTICE

7B Months and ordinals

1 ▶ 7.5 Listen and repeat.

1 January	2 February	3 March	4 April
5 May	6 June	7 July	8 August
9 September	10 October	11 November	12 December

2 ▶ 7.6 Listen and repeat.

1st	first	7th	seventh	13th	thirteenth	19th	nineteenth
2nd	second	8th	eighth	14th	fourteenth	20th	twentieth
3rd	third	9th	ninth	15th	fifteenth	21st	twenty-first
4th	fourth	10th	tenth	16th	sixteenth	22nd	twenty-second
5th	fifth	11th	eleventh	17th	seventeenth	30th	thirtieth
6th	sixth	12th	twelfth	18th	eighteenth	31st	thirty-first

> **Look!** In American English, the ordinal comes after the month.
>
> *February 2 = February second*
> *June 16 = June sixteenth*

3 Look at the dates in parentheses and complete the sentences with the words.

1 Valentine's Day is _____ _____ . (2/14)
2 Independence Day in the U.S. is _____ _____ . (7/4)
3 New Year's Day is _____ _____ . (1/1)

4 Veterans Day is _____ _____ . (11/11)
5 My birthday is _____ _____ . (7/25)
6 Cinco de Mayo is _____ _____ . (5/5)

◀ Go back to page 62

7C Time expressions

1 ▶ 7.14 Listen and repeat.

1 last   last night, last week, last year
2 ago   two days ago, three weeks ago, four years ago
3 yesterday   yesterday morning, yesterday afternoon, yesterday evening
4 times   at 9:00, at 11:30, at midnight
5 days   on Monday, on Tuesdays, on the weekend
6 dates   on January 1, on April 24, on December 11
7 years   in 1985, in 2001, in 2018
8 decades   in the 1960s, in the 1990s, in the 2010s

2 Complete the sentences with the words in the box.

> on (x2)   in   ago   last (x2)   yesterday   at

1 I studied English _____ morning. Then I watched TV.
2 We enjoyed your party _____ night. It was great!
3 Samantha meets her friends _____ 6:30 after work.
4 I lived in Madrid _____ the 1980s. It was an interesting time.

5 My brother traveled to Europe _____ year.
6 I started my new job _____ November 4.
7 My grandmother was a teacher 50 years _____ .
8 I usually finish work early _____ Fridays.

124

◀ Go back to page 65

VOCABULARY PRACTICE

8A Travel verbs

1 ▶ 8.1 Listen and repeat.

1 **book** a flight

2 **fly**

3 **get in** a taxi

4 **get lost**

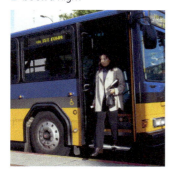
5 **get off** a bus

6 **get on** a train

7 **get out of** a taxi

8 **miss** the bus

9 **ride** a bike

10 **sail**

11 **take** the subway

12 **walk**

2 Check (✓) the verbs we can use with each type of transportation.

	a taxi	a bike	a boat	a plane	a bus	a train
ride						
take						
miss						
get in / out of						
get on / off						
sail						

3 Choose the correct words to complete the sentences.

1 Anne needs to *walk / book* a ticket for her trip to Los Angeles.
2 This is our bus stop. Quick, *get off / get out* now!
3 Let's *walk / get out* home. It's a nice warm evening.
4 Juan decided to *sail / fly* to Spain because he hates planes.
5 When the train arrived, a lot of people tried to *get lost / get on*.
6 There are no trains. We need to *ride / take* a taxi home.
7 They *missed / booked* their bus, so they arrived really late.
8 I can drive you home if you want. *Get in / Get out*!
9 Stuart *drives / rides* a motorcycle because it's fast.
10 You can *take / fly* the number 35 bus downtown.

◀ Go back to page 68

VOCABULARY PRACTICE

8B Weather and seasons

1 ▶ 8.6 Listen and repeat.

1 hot
2 warm
3 cold
4 cloudy
5 sunny
6 wet
7 dry
8 windy
9 foggy
10 rain
11 snow
12 spring
13 summer
14 fall
15 winter

Look! *rain* and *snow* are verbs. To talk about the weather now, we say *It's raining/It's snowing*. To talk about the weather in general, we say *It rains/It snows*.

2 Look at the weather map and complete the sentences.

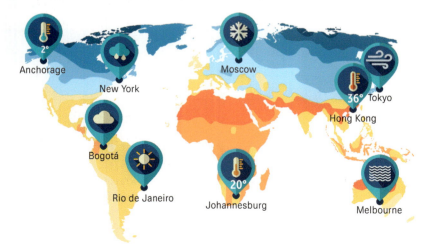

1 It's _____ in Moscow.
2 It's _____ in Bogotá.
3 It's _____ in Rio de Janeiro.
4 It's _____ in New York.
5 It's _____ in Tokyo.
6 It's _____ in Hong Kong.
7 It's _____ in Anchorage.
8 It's _____ in Johannesburg.
9 It's _____ in Melbourne.

◀ Go back to page 70

VOCABULARY PRACTICE

8C Nature

1 ▶ 8.7 Listen and repeat.

1 beach

2 cloud

3 field

4 flower

5 forest

6 grass

7 mountain

8 ocean

9 river

10 sky

11 sun

12 tree

2 Choose the correct words to complete the sentences.
1 Kilimanjaro is a *beach* / *mountain* in Tanzania.
2 The Nile is a *river* / *field* in Africa.
3 The Amazon is a *forest* / *mountain* in South America.
4 The rose is a *cloud* / *flower* that can be different colors.
5 Bermuda is in the Atlantic *Ocean* / *River*.
6 Copacabana is a *beach* / *forest* in Brazil.
7 Apples are a fruit that come from a *grass* / *tree*.
8 The temperature of the *sun* / *sky* is 15 million °C.
9 Cumulus, cirrus, and stratus are *clouds* / *trees*.
10 Animals like horses and rabbits eat *trees* / *grass*.

◀ Go back to page 72

> **VOCABULARY PRACTICE**

9A Clothes

1 ▶ 9.1 Listen and repeat.

1 belt
2 boots
3 coat
4 dress
5 hat
6 jacket
7 jeans
8 pants
9 shirt
10 shoes
11 skirt
12 socks
13 suit
14 sweater
15 T-shirt

2 Write the clothes from exercise 1 in the correct places.

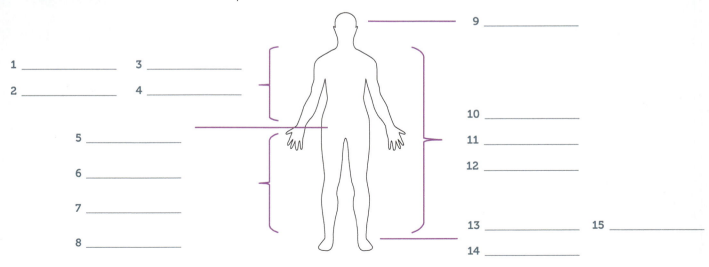

1 _____
2 _____
3 _____
4 _____
5 _____
6 _____
7 _____
8 _____
9 _____
10 _____
11 _____
12 _____
13 _____
14 _____
15 _____

◀ Go back to page 78

VOCABULARY PRACTICE

9B Feelings

1 ▶ 9.6 Listen and repeat.

 1 angry
 2 bored
 3 calm
 4 excited

 5 happy
 6 hungry
 7 sad
 8 scared

 9 surprised
 10 thirsty
 11 tired
 12 worried

2 Choose the correct adjective to complete the sentences.

1 Can I have a glass of water? I'm really *hungry / thirsty*.
2 He's *surprised / worried* about money because he doesn't have a job.
3 I'm *bored / scared*. This movie's not very interesting.
4 It's Louisa's birthday tomorrow – she's very *excited / tired*.
5 I like yoga because it makes me feel *calm / sad*.
6 Are you *angry / hungry*? Do you want a sandwich?
7 You're very *scared / tired*. Why don't you go to bed?
8 Tim is *angry / hungry* with me because I broke his computer.
9 I was *bored / surprised* that John ran a marathon because he doesn't like sports.
10 Suzie doesn't like horror movies. They make her feel *scared / surprised*.

3 Match the feelings in the box with the messages.

| tired   sad   worried   angry   surprised |

1 **Julia** I get my grades today! 😬
2 **Ying-Li** I arrived in Chicago today after a 10-hour flight. 😴
3 **Saanvi** I won the science competition. I can't believe it! 😱
4 **Dave** All my friends are in Hawaii on vacation. I'm at work. 😣
5 **Hans** I lost my wallet on the train today … and I was late for work. 😠

◀ Go back to page 80

129

VOCABULARY PRACTICE

9C Shopping

1 ▶ 9.12 Listen and repeat.

1 buy a car

2 go shopping

3 pay by credit card

4 pay with cash

5 sell ice cream

6 shop online

7 spend money

8 try on clothes

9 department store

10 local stores

11 market

12 shopping mall

2 Match the sentence parts to make full sentences.

1 I always pay by
2 We usually spend
3 Can I try on
4 I never shop
5 Jorge sells
6 Malika wants to buy
7 You can only pay with
8 We need to go

a these jeans, please?
b a new laptop.
c fish in the market.
d grocery shopping.
e $100 every weekend.
f credit card. It's easy!
g cash in this store.
h online. I like real stores.

3 Choose the correct words to complete the sentences.

1 I don't *go / buy* shopping on Saturdays. There are lots of people.
2 My brother works for a technology company. He *spends / sells* computers.
3 Sharon lives in a small town. There are only three or four *department stores / local stores*.
4 Carla *spends / buys* all her money on clothes.
5 When we go on vacation, we usually pay *with / by* credit card.
6 The *shopping mall / market* near us has a movie theater and lots of restaurants.
7 I always *try / shop* on clothes before I buy them.
8 My cell phone is broken. I need to *buy / pay* a new one.

◀ Go back to page 82

VOCABULARY PRACTICE

10A Free-time activities

1 ▶ 10.1 Listen and repeat.

1 go to a concert

2 go to a festival

3 go to the beach

4 have a barbecue

5 have a good time

6 have a party

7 stay at a hotel

8 stay home

9 stay in a tent

10 visit a museum

11 visit an art gallery

12 visit family/friends

13 watch a movie

14 watch a soccer game

15 watch a video

2 Match the activities in the box with the people.

> visit family   go to the beach   have a barbecue   watch a movie
> have a party   stay home   visit a museum   stay in a tent

1 Erica likes hot weather and swimming. She has two new books to read. _____
2 It's a beautiful sunny day. Paul is hungry, and he has some meat and fish. _____
3 It's Lucia's birthday tomorrow, and she wants to celebrate with her friends. _____
4 The weather's not good, and Samuel has an exam next week. _____
5 Marek and Kasia are in Charleston for the weekend. They're interested in history. _____
6 Sonia loves nature. She wants to go on vacation, but she doesn't want to spend a lot of money. _____
7 Cristian is going to San Francisco. His family lives there. _____
8 Natalia is at home tonight. She bought a new 40-inch TV last week. _____

◀ Go back to page 86

VOCABULARY PRACTICE

10B Types of music and movies

1 ▶ 10.9 Listen and repeat.

 1 classical music
 2 electronic music
 3 hip-hop music
 4 jazz music

 5 pop music
 6 rock music
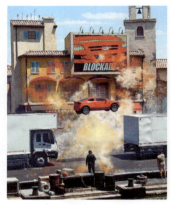 7 an action movie
 8 a comedy

 9 a drama
 10 a horror movie
 11 a romance
 12 a science-fiction movie

2 Look at the pictures and write the types of music and movies.

 1 _____
 2 _____
 3 _____
 4 _____
 5 _____
 6 _____

132   ◀ Go back to page 88

VOCABULARY PRACTICE

10C Sports and games

1 ▶ 10.10 Listen and repeat.

1 do gymnastics   2 do karate   3 do pilates   4 do yoga

5 go bike riding   6 go hiking   7 go rock climbing   8 go running

9 go skiing   10 go swimming   11 play baseball   12 play basketball

13 play chess   14 play hockey   15 play soccer   16 play tennis

17 play videogames   18 play volleyball

> **Look!**
> We use *play* with sports that use a ball and with games.
> *I play golf.*
> We use *go* with activities that end in *-ing*.
> *I go sailing.*
> We use *do* with individual activities and sports that don't use a ball.
> *I do judo.*

2 Complete the sentences with the correct form of *go*, *play*, or *do*.

1 He usually _____ tennis on the weekend.
2 It's a beautiful sunny day. Why don't we _____ hiking?
3 They _____ gymnastics every Monday after school.
4 Do you want to _____ chess later?
5 Did you _____ bike riding last weekend?
6 She often _____ pilates to relax.
7 I _____ skiing with my parents every winter.
8 Do your children _____ a lot of videogames?

◀ Go back to page 90

133

COMMUNICATION PRACTICE

6A Student A

Look at the picture. Ask and answer questions with Student B to find six differences.

A *Are there any hotels?*
B *Yes, there are. There are two hotels.*
A *In my picture, there's one hotel.*
B *Is there a movie theater?*

6C Student A

1 Describe your picture to Student B. He/She will draw it.

A *There's a bed. Next to the bed, there's a small table.*

2 Listen to Student B and draw the room.

B *There's a sofa in front of the window.*

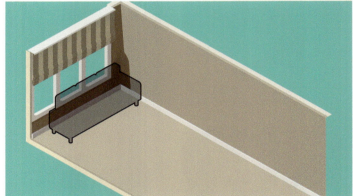

138

COMMUNICATION PRACTICE

6D Student A

1 Ask Student B for directions to the places in the box. Listen and mark on the map where they are. Check the information if you need to.

> post office   bank   Internet café

A *Excuse me, is there a post office near here?*
B *Yes, there is. You go down Market Street …*
A *Could you repeat that, please?*

2 Listen to Student B. Look at the map and give directions.

7A Student A

1 Ask Student B questions with *was* to match the famous people with their jobs and where they were from.

A *Was Federico Fellini an artist?*
B *No, he wasn't.*

1 Federico Fellini	writer	South Africa
2 Janis Joplin	politician	the U.S.
3 Nelson Mandela	movie director	Colombia
4 Greta Garbo	artist	Japan
5 Katsushika Hokusai	singer	Italy
6 Gabriel García Márquez	actor	Sweden

2 Answer Student B's questions about the famous people. You can only say *Yes, he/she was* or *No, he/she wasn't*.

1 Frida Kahlo was an artist from Mexico.
2 Johan Cruyff was a soccer player from the Netherlands.
3 Celia Cruz was a singer from Cuba.
4 Jane Austen was a writer from the UK.
5 Paco de Lucía was a musician from Spain.
6 Jawaharlal Nehru was a politician from India.

7C Student A

1 Ask Student B questions. Find one incorrect piece of information for each person.

A *Did Luke visit his grandparents last week?*
B *No, he didn't. He visited his grandparents last month.*

1 Luke / visit / his grandparents / last ~~week~~   month
2 Kenny / travel / to Brazil / three years ago
3 Clara / play / volleyball / yesterday
4 Debbie / cook / noodles / last night
5 Steve / work / as a teacher / in the 1980s
6 Amelia / watch / a TV show / yesterday morning

2 Listen to Student B's questions. Correct the information.

1 Zoe stayed at a hotel downtown last year.
2 Jim studied Spanish in college in the 1990s.
3 Antonia walked 18 miles yesterday.
4 Leandro watched a soccer game three days ago.
5 Rachel started a new job in London last month.
6 Tom finished work one hour ago.

7A London's famous houses: answers

1 Mahatma Gandhi

2 Bob Marley

3 Agatha Christie

4 Vincent van Gogh

139

COMMUNICATION PRACTICE

8A Student A

1 Ask Student B questions to find out what Lola did yesterday.

A *Where did Lola go?*
B *She went to her dad's birthday party.*

2 Read the information and answer Student B's questions about what Mateo did yesterday.

Lola	Where / go?
	What time / leave / the house?
	she / take / the bus?
	What / wear?
	What / buy / for her dad?
	she / have / a good time?
	Where / sleep / last night?

Mateo	He / go / Rome
	He / fly
	He / take / taxi to the airport
	His flight / leave at 11:00 a.m.
	He / go / with friends
	He / sleep / on a plane for 20 minutes
	He / have / a good trip

8C Student A

1 Look at the picture for one minute. Then close your book and answer Student B's questions.

2 Give Student B one minute to look at his/her picture. Ask him/her questions with *Was/Were there a/an/any …?* and the words in the box. If he/she answers *Yes, there were*, ask *How many were there?*

| boats | hospital | cars | flowers |
| birds | stores | beach | river |

A *Were there any boats?*   B *Yes, there were.*
A *How many were there?*   B *There was one boat.*

8D Student A

1 Read the situation in the box, and then look at the flowchart. You are the receptionist. Student B calls you. Have the conversation.

A *Hello, Green Lane Medical Center. Jorge speaking. How can I help you?*
B *Hello, my name's Anna Lopez. I'd like to see the doctor.*

> You work at the Green Lane Medical Center. Answer the phone. Ask the person what the problem is.

Receptionist

- Answer the phone. Give the name of the medical center/sports center and your name.
- Ask more detailed questions.
- Ask for the caller's contact details.
- Finish the call.

Patient/Customer

- Introduce yourself and say why you are calling.
- Answer.
- Answer.

2 Read the situation in the box, and then look at the flowchart again. You are the customer. Call Student B and have the conversation.

> You want to join a sports center. You're interested in swimming and tennis. Your phone number is 555-1212.

140

COMMUNICATION PRACTICE

9C   Student A

Ask and answer the question *How often do/does ...?* with Student B to complete the chart.

A *How often do Jon and Andy go to the movies?*
B *They go to the movies three or four times a year.*

Laura	have dinner in a restaurant	twice a month
Jon and Andy	go to the movies	
Carlota	shop online	once or twice a week
Ahmed	ride a motorcycle	
Hope and Sara	check their e-mails	four or five times a day
Igor	read a new book	
Luisa and Raul	go swimming	every week
Yannis	go on vacation	

10A   Student A

Look at your schedule. Try to find a time when you can meet Student B. Ask and answer the question *What are you doing on ...?* for the different days.

A *What are you doing on Monday morning?*
B *I'm going to the gym. What about Monday afternoon?*

	Monday	Tuesday	Wednesday	Thursday	Friday
Morning			travel to the city		
Afternoon	see doctor	have lunch with parents	visit National Museum		
Evening	watch movie at movie theater		stay with friends		have dinner with Carl

10C   Student A

Ask Student B questions about his/her hobby in the correct tense. Write down his/her answers. Then guess what the hobby is.

A *How often do you do your hobby?*
B *I do it twice a week.*

Student B's hobby

Your hobby: rock climbing

1	How often / you / do / your hobby?	Every weekend.
2	When / you / start?	When I was 14.
3	it / be / expensive?	No, it's not.
4	it / be / dangerous?	It can be.
5	you / play / it in a team?	No, but I always go with another person.
6	How many people / be there / in your team?	–
7	Where / you / do / your hobby?	Sometimes at a sports center, sometimes in the mountains.
8	you / do / your hobby next weekend?	Yes, I'm driving to the beach on Friday night.

141

COMMUNICATION PRACTICE

6A Student B

Look at the picture. Ask and answer questions with Student A to find six differences.

B *Are there any hotels?*
A *Yes, there are. There's one hotel.*
B *In my picture, there are two hotels.*
A *Is there a movie theater?*

6C Student B

1 Listen to Student A and draw the room.

A *There's a bed. Next to the bed, there's a small table.*

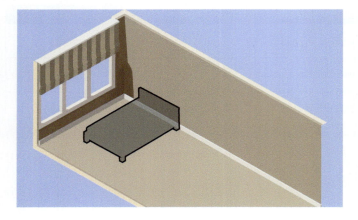

2 Describe your picture to Student A. He/She will draw it.

B *There's a sofa in front of the window.*

COMMUNICATION PRACTICE

6D Student B

1 Listen to Student A. Look at the map and give directions.

   A *Excuse me, is there a post office near here?*
   B *Yes, there is. You go down Market Street …*
   A *Could you repeat that, please?*

2 Ask Student A for directions to the places in the box. Listen and mark on the map where they are. Check the information if you need to.

   restaurant
   tourist information office
   grocery store

7A Student B

1 Answer Student A's questions about the famous people. You can only say *Yes, he/she was* or *No, he/she wasn't*.

   A *Was Federico Fellini an artist?*
   B *No, he wasn't.*
   1 Federico Fellini was a movie director from Italy.
   2 Janis Joplin was a singer from the U.S.
   3 Nelson Mandela was a politician from South Africa.
   4 Greta Garbo was an actor from Sweden.
   5 Katsushika Hokusai was an artist from Japan.
   6 Gabriel García Márquez was a writer from Colombia.

2 Ask Student A questions with *was* to match the famous people with their jobs and where they were from.

   1 Frida Kahlo   soccer player   India
   2 Johan Cruyff   musician   Spain
   3 Celia Cruz   politician   Mexico
   4 Jane Austen   singer   the Netherlands
   5 Paco de Lucía   writer   Cuba
   6 Jawaharlal Nehru   artist   the UK

7C Student B

1 Listen to Student A's questions. Correct the information.

   A *Did Luke visit his grandparents last week?*
   B *No, he didn't. He visited his grandparents last month.*
   1 Luke visited his grandparents last month.
   2 Kenny traveled to Brazil six years ago.
   3 Clara played basketball yesterday.
   4 Debbie cooked rice last night.
   5 Steve worked as a teacher in the 1970s.
   6 Amelia watched a movie yesterday morning.

2 Ask Student A questions. Find one incorrect piece of information for each person.

   1 Zoe / stay / at a hotel near the beach / last year
   2 Jim / study / German in college / in the 1990s
   3 Antonia / walk / 18 miles / two days ago
   4 Leandro / watch / a soccer game / last week
   5 Rachel / start / a new job in Paris / last month
   6 Tom / finish / work / half an hour ago

9C Questionnaire results

Mostly as: You don't like shopping, and you hate shopping malls. You prefer to spend money on other things. What do you do and how often do you do it?

Mostly bs: You like shopping, but you also like doing other things. A shopping mall is a good place to meet friends. How often do you go there?

Mostly cs: You love shopping – it's your life. You go shopping two or three times a week, and you shop online almost every day … but do you really need to buy all those things?

147

COMMUNICATION PRACTICE

8A Student B

1 Read the information and answer Student A's questions about what Lola did yesterday.

A *Where did Lola go?* **B** *She went to her dad's birthday party.*

Lola	She / go / her dad's birthday party
	She / leave / the house at 7:00 p.m.
	She / take / the train
	She / wear / a new dress
	She / buy / a book
	She / have / a good time
	She / sleep / on her dad's sofa

2 Ask Student A questions to find out what Mateo did yesterday.

Mateo	Where / he / go?
	he / go / by train?
	he / take / a taxi to the airport?
	What time / his flight / leave?
	he / go / with friends?
	he / sleep / on the plane?
	he / have / a good trip?

8C Student B

1 Give Student A one minute to look at his/her picture. Ask him/her questions with *Was/Were there a/an/any …?* and the words in the box. If he/she answers *Yes, there were*, ask *How many were there?*

| people   clouds   forest   trees |
| bus   houses   cars   river |

B *Were there any people?* **A** *Yes, there were.*
B *How many were there?* **A** *There were four people.*

2 Look at the picture for one minute. Then close your book and answer Student A's questions.

8D Student B

1 Read the situation in the box, and then look at the flowchart. You are the patient. Call Student A and have the conversation.

A *Hello, Green Lane Medical Center. Jorge speaking. How can I help you?*
B *Hello, my name's Anna Lopez. I'd like to see the doctor.*

> You don't feel well and want to see the doctor. Your head hurts. Your phone number is 951-742-5061.

Receptionist

- Answer the phone. Give the name of the medical center/sports center and your name.
- Ask more detailed questions.
- Ask for the caller's contact details.
- Finish the call.

Patient/Customer

- Introduce yourself and say why you are calling.
- Answer.
- Answer.

2 Read the situation in the box, and then look at the flowchart again. You are the receptionist. Student A calls you. Have the conversation.

> You work at a sports center called The Fitness Factory. Answer the phone. Ask the person what sports they want to play.

COMMUNICATION PRACTICE

9A Student B

Look at the picture. Describe James, Grace, and Kara to Student A. Try to find six differences.

B *Grace is wearing a red dress and boots.*
A *In my picture, she's wearing shoes.*

9C Student B

Ask and answer the question *How often do/does …?* with Student A to complete the chart.

B *How often does Laura have dinner in a restaurant?*
A *She has dinner in a restaurant twice a month.*

Laura	have dinner in a restaurant	
Jon and Andy	go to the movies	three or four times a year
Carlota	shop online	
Ahmed	ride a motorcycle	every day
Hope and Sara	check their e-mails	
Igor	read a new book	four or five times a year
Luisa and Raul	go swimming	
Yannis	go on vacation	once a year

10A Student B

Look at your schedule. Try to find a time when you can meet Student A. Ask and answer the question *What are you doing on …?* for the different days.

A *What are you doing on Monday morning?*
B *I'm going to the gym. What about Monday afternoon?*

	Monday	Tuesday	Wednesday	Thursday	Friday
Morning	go to the gym	meet Simon for coffee		take bus to city	see dentist
Afternoon				visit art gallery	
Evening		go to a concert		stay at hotel	

COMMUNICATION PRACTICE

9A Student A

Look at the picture. Describe Aziz, Oscar, and Petra to Student B. Try to find six differences.

A *Aziz is looking at a white hat.*
B *In my picture, he's looking at some sunglasses.*

10C Student B

Ask Student A questions about his/her hobby in the correct tense. Write down his/her answers. Then guess what the hobby is.

B *How often do you do your hobby?*
A *I do it every weekend.*

	Student A's hobby	Your hobby: basketball
1 How often / you / do / your hobby?		Twice a week.
2 When / you / start?		Last year.
3 it / be / expensive?		No, it's not.
4 it / be / dangerous?		No, it's not.
5 you / play / it in a team?		Yes, I do.
6 How many people / be there / in your team?		12 (but only five play at the same time).
7 Where / you / do / your hobby?		At the sports center.
8 you / do / your hobby next weekend?		Yes, we're going to Los Angeles for a game.

10D Students A and B

1 Complete the sentences. You can use real information or invent it.

About me
In my free time, I often _____ .
My favorite type of music is _____ .
Last weekend
I went shopping on Saturday, and I bought _____
_____ .
Last weekend, I _____ .

My vacations
Last summer, I went to _____ .
When I'm on vacation, I usually _____ .
My plans
Next weekend, I'm meeting _____ .
For my next vacation, I'm _____ .

2 Read your sentences in pairs. Respond with interest using the words in the box.

Oh really?   That's interesting.   That sounds good.   Wow, that's awesome!   Cool!   Great!

A *In my free time, I often go skiing in the mountains.*
B *Wow, that's awesome!*

Irregular verbs

Infinitive	Simple past
be	was, were
become	became
begin	began
break	broke
bring	brought
buy	bought
choose	chose
come	came
cost	cost
do	did
drink	drank
drive	drove
eat	ate
fall	fell
feel	felt
find	found
fly	flew
get	got
give	gave
go	went
have	had
hear	heard
hold	held
hurt	hurt
keep	kept
know	knew

Infinitive	Simple past
leave	left
lose	lost
make	made
meet	met
pay	paid
put	put
read (/riːd/)	read (/red/)
ride	rode
run	ran
say	said
see	saw
sell	sold
sit	sat
sleep	slept
spend	spent
speak	spoke
stand	stood
swim	swam
take	took
teach	taught
tell	told
think	thought
understand	understood
wake	woke
wear	wore
win	won
write	wrote

American English

Personal Best

Workbook — A1 Beginner

Richmond

UNIT 6 Places

6A LANGUAGE

GRAMMAR: there is/are

1 ▶6.1 Complete the conversation with the words in the box. Listen and check.

there are some (3)   there's an
are there any   is there a   there are no
is there an   there's no (3)   there aren't

A In this picture, ¹ _there are some_ pencils.
B ² _____ pen.
A ³ _____ book? No …
B ⁴ But _____ glasses. Reading glasses.
A ⁵ _____ sunglasses.
B But ⁶ _____ umbrella.
A ⁷ _____ wallet.
B ⁸ _____ credit cards?
A Credit cards? No, ⁹ _____.
B ¹⁰ _____ key? Yes, one.
A ¹¹ _____ camera.
B But ¹² _____ cell phones – two!

2 Read the information about Nuuk, the capital of Greenland. Then complete the text with *there is/there are*, and *a/an*, *some*, *any*, or *no*.

population	17,000	shopping malls	1
airports	1	cafés & restaurants	10+
schools	5+	art galleries	?
big hotels	1	clubs	?
roads out of town	0	boats and ferries	100s!
parks	0		

Nuuk is the capital of Greenland, but it only has 17,000 people. ¹ _There's an_ airport and ² _____ schools. ³ _____ big hotel, but ⁴ _____ roads out of Nuuk and ⁵ _____ parks. ⁶ _____ shopping mall and ⁷ _____ cafés and restaurants. ⁸ _____ art gallery? I don't think so. What about clubs? ⁹ _____ clubs? I'm not sure. But I know that ¹⁰ _____ boats and ferries – lots of them!

VOCABULARY: Places in a town

3 Order the letters to make places in a town.

1 s t o p f e c i o f   p_____ o_____
2 h a i l s p o t   h_____
3 v i o m e r t e a h t e m_____ t_____
4 b u l c   c_____
5 l e p i c o n a t t o s i p_____ s_____
6 y g c e o r r r s e o t g_____ s_____
7 r a n t i o s t i n a t t_____ s_____
8 u s e m u m   m_____

4 Complete the sentences with places in a town.

1 buy clothes, computers, sunglasses, books, etc. in a s_____ m_____
2 catch the bus at the b_____ s_____
3 eat in a c_____ or r_____
4 keep your money in a b_____
5 sleep in a h_____
6 catch a plane from the a_____
7 walk your dog in the p_____
8 learn English at a language s_____

PRONUNCIATION: Linking consonants and vowels

5 ▶6.2 Listen and repeat the sentences. Pay attention to how the sounds link together.

1 There‿are some cafés.
2 There's‿a restaurant.
3 Is there‿a shopping mall?
4 Yes, there‿is. There‿are two schools, too.
5 There‿are eight‿stores.
6 There‿is a post‿office.
7 Are there‿any parks?
8 No, there‿aren't.

34

SKILLS 6B

READING: Reading in detail

1 Read the article. Who thinks the city is a good place to live – Ursula or Lenny? Who thinks the country is a good place to live? Whose opinion do you agree with, Ursula's or Lenny's?

BIG CITY or COUNTRY?

Where is a better place to live? We ask two friends to give their opinions.

Ursula Is life exciting in the city? In my view, traveling an hour to work every day is not exciting. Also, it's not expensive in the country. Small apartments in big cities are expensive.

People say that it's boring here because it's difficult to find things to do. But I like going for walks and learning about animals and birds. There's lots to do in the city, but I don't think theaters and museums are interesting.

Finally, people are friendly in the country. We say "hi" to everyone. Not like in cities!

Lenny The country is a great place to live ... if you like to drive! Why live in a place where you need a car because the movie theater is 20 miles away?

Also, there are no good jobs and the only social life is online. In my opinion, cities are interesting for young people because everything you need is right there.

Also, you don't need a car because you can walk or ride a bike. So city life is good for you and the planet.

2 Read the article again. Choose yes (Y) or no (N). Write the word or phrase in the article that gives you the answer. Use the underlined key words to help you.

1 Does Ursula know Lenny? (Y) / N _friends_
2 Does Ursula think life is exciting in the city? Y / N _____
3 Are there many things to do in the city, in Ursula's opinion? Y / N _____
4 In Ursula's opinion, are cities unfriendly? Y / N _____
5 Does Lenny say cars are necessary in the country? Y / N _____
6 Does Lenny think the country is good for young people? Y / N _____
7 Does Lenny like to have movie theaters, grocery stores, etc. near him? Y / N _____

3 Match the two parts of the sentences.

1 Ursula doesn't like ____   a cities are boring.
2 She doesn't think that the ____   b good places to live.
3 She likes ____   c going for walks.
4 Lenny doesn't think ____   d interesting things to do in cities.
5 He thinks there are ____   e long trips to work.
6 In his view, cities are ____   f country is boring.

4 Complete the parts of the body.

1 It's easy to see where something is with two e___ ___ on the front of our f___ ___ ___.
2 Our e___ ___ ___ are on the side of our h___ ___ ___.
3 There are 32 t___ ___ ___ in an adult's m___ ___ ___ ___, but only 20 in a child's.
4 Your h___ ___ ___ and f___ ___ ___ are at the end of your arms and legs.
5 Our h___ ___ ___ helps to keep us warm!
6 We use our n___ ___ ___ to smell things like food.
7 You can look after your b___ ___ ___ by eating healthy food and exercising.
8 Running long distances can be bad for your k___ ___ ___ ___.

35

6C LANGUAGE

GRAMMAR: Prepositions of place

1 Choose the correct prepositions to complete the sentences.

1 My pen is _____ your chair. Can you give it to me?
   a between   b in   c under
2 The children's bedroom is very small, so they have "bunk beds" – one bed is _____ the other.
   a above   b next to   c behind
3 I think that new lamp looks good _____ the computer and the window.
   a on   b under   c between
4 We have a bed, a chair, and a table _____ our bedroom.
   a in   b above   c next to
5 Why is the television _____ the desk? We can't watch a movie like that!
   a in front of   b between   c behind
6 There's a beautiful park _____ our apartment. You can see it from our living room.
   a above   b in front of   c in
7 Please put the salad _____ the table for our lunch.
   a on   b under   c next to
8 The train station is _____ the stores. Go through the shopping mall and you can see it on the other side.
   a under   b behind   c above

2 Complete the sentences with the correct prepositions.

1 Come and sit _____ to me. We can do our homework together.
2 Please don't stand in _____ of the refrigerator. I need the milk and some eggs.
3 I can't see my car – it's _____ the house. But I'm sure it's there!
4 He keeps his keys _____ his wallet so he doesn't lose them.
5 It's raining. Do you want to stand _____ my umbrella with me?
6 Is the club _____ the movie theater and the bank?
7 Planes fly _____ our town all day. It's very noisy sometimes!
8 Don't put your dirty feet _____ the table!

VOCABULARY: Rooms and furniture

3 Look at the words in the box. Order the letters then write the words in the correct rooms.

| ~~deb~~ | fosa | vetso | herows |
| bhabtut | ittelo | lcteso | |

bedroom	bathroom
bed	_____
_____	_____
_____	_____

kitchen	living room
_____	_____

4 Look at the picture. Complete the description.

This is my ¹_____. I do my homework here. I have my laptop on this ²_____. There's a large ³_____ above it, so I have lots of light in the day. But in the evening, I turn on my ⁴_____ next to the computer. I have lots of books, so there are some long ⁵_____ between the desk and the ⁶_____ with my coffee cup. My ⁷_____ is big but old, so I sometimes sit on the sofa to study. But my favorite thing? I have a small ⁸_____ under my desk with cold drinks and chocolate. It's my mini-kitchen!

PRONUNCIATION: Sentence stress

5 ▶ 6.3 Underline the stressed words. Listen and check.

1 My desk is under the window.
2 The table is next to the shelves.
3 Their bathroom is above the kitchen.
4 The chair is between the bed and the closet.
5 His keys are on the chair.
6 Our sofa is in the living room.

SKILLS 6D

SPEAKING: Asking for and giving directions

1 ▶ 6.4 Listen to three conversations. Where do the people want to go?

1 The woman wants to go to the _____.
2 The man wants to go to the _____.
3 The man wants to go to the _____.

2 ▶ 6.4 Listen again and complete the conversations.

Conversation 1

1 _____ me, _____ the park, please?

2 Go _____ this street and turn _____ at the hospital.

Conversation 2

3 Is _____ a police station around _____?

4 _____ right just before the post office. You can see it _____ the post office, on the _____.

Conversation 3

5 Is the museum _____ here?

6 Go down _____ street for about three or four _____ and then turn right _____ the shopping mall.

3 ▶ 6.5 Listen to the conversation. Which place does the man call?

a the post office
b the movie theater
c the swimming pool

4 ▶ 6.6 Listen again to six extracts from the conversation in exercise 3. Match each extract with the ways of checking information (a–c).

1 ____
2 ____
3 ____
4 ____
5 ____
6 ____

a asking someone to repeat
b asking someone to speak more slowly
c asking a question to check the information

37

6 REVIEW and PRACTICE

HOME   BLOG   **PODCASTS**   ABOUT   CONTACT

Tom and Sam talk about Brad's house.

LISTENING

1 ▶ **6.7** Listen to the podcast about a very small house. Check (✔) the things Brad has in his house.

a   stove   _____
b   table   _____
c   sofa   _____
d   chair   _____
e   desk   _____
f   bathtub   _____
g   shower   _____
h   toilet   _____
i   closet   _____
j   bed   _____

2 ▶ **6.7** Listen again. Write T (true), F (false), or NG (not given) if there is no information in the podcast.

1   Tom says that Sam has lots of parties.   _____
2   There are thirteen small houses near Brad.   _____
3   Brad has a large yard at the front of his house.   _____
4   Brad cooks every day.   _____
5   There are four chairs in the living room.   _____
6   Brad's friends visit him on Saturdays.   _____
7   Brad prefers showers to baths.   _____
8   Brad's bed is in the closet.   _____
9   Brad pays $600 each month for his house.   _____
10 Brad wants to live in a different house when he is older.   _____

READING

1 Read Penny's blog about New York. Choose the correct sentence.

a   The three places are all free.
b   You can see art at all these places.
c   All the places are very old.

2 Read the blog again. Match the sentences with places a–c.

1   Some visitors don't know it's there.   _____
2   This place is new and also free.   _____
3   There are good places to eat here.   _____
4   You can see movies here.   _____
5   It's easy to go there by bus.   _____
6   There are beautiful views when you walk here.   _____

a   the High Line   b   the Cloisters
c   Williamsburg

3 Complete the sentences with places in a town.

1   Is there a p _ _ _ o _ _ _ _ e near here? I need to buy some stamps.
2   Daisy broke her leg and had to go to the h _ _ _ _ _ _ l.
3   Let's go to a c _ _ _ this evening and go dancing!
4   Can you go to the g _ _ _ _ _ y s _ _ _ _ and buy some bread and milk, please?
5   Shall we get our tickets online or from the t _ _ _ _ s _ _ _ _ _ n?
6   We stayed at a really expensive h_ _ _ l when we visited Barcelona.
7   I usually buy presents at the s _ _ _ _ _ _ g m _ _ _ in town.
8   Nick left his wallet on the bus and had to go to the p _ _ _ _ e s _ _ _ _ _ n.
9   Which s _ _ _ _ l do his children go to?
10 I spent all my money, so I went to the b _ _ k to get some more.

38

REVIEW and PRACTICE 6

HOME **BLOG** PODCASTS ABOUT CONTACT

This week's guest blogger Penny writes about the New York hosts' favorite places.

Enjoying the "Big Apple"

At the New York studio, we're really lucky to live in a fantastic city with lots to see and do. There are many parks and museums and there are so many restaurants and cafés. It's not easy to choose, but I want to tell you about our favorite places in the city.

Penny

My favorite place is the High Line, a new park in Midtown Manhattan. Before, it was a train line, but now it is a park above the city, about a mile long. I love walking, and this is a great place to walk. And there are amazing views of the city and the Hudson River. There are also many plants and flowers to look at on the way, and some very good street art, all free. There are lots of different entrances but the easiest for me is between 11th and 12th Avenues on 34th Street. I often go on the weekend, when I have time.

I love a museum called the Cloisters, in northern Manhattan. Not many tourists know about it, and it is pretty far from downtown. But it's easy to travel there because there is a bus stop next to it. It's about $25 to get in, so I don't go very often. But it's fantastic! At the center is a really old building and there's lots of interesting old art to see. And there are some beautiful gardens in front of the castle. I like going there because it's very quiet.

Ethan

Marc

On the weekend, I sometimes go to Williamsburg in Brooklyn. It's an exciting part of the city, where you can go to fantastic cafés or just walk around the markets and enjoy the atmosphere. I love looking at the street art. There is also a great movie theater on Grand Street. There are seven screens and seats for nearly 1,000 people! People from all over the world live in Williamsburg, and everyone is really friendly. If you want to go shopping, it's great for fresh food and old clothes

These are our favorite places, but what about you? Tell us about your favorite places in your city!

UNIT 7 All in the past

7A — LANGUAGE

GRAMMAR: Simple past: *be*

1 Complete the sentences with *was*, *were*, *wasn't*, or *weren't*.

1 Where _____ you on Tuesday?

2 Oh, good. You have your cell phone. Where _____ it?

3 The movie _____ very good. Don't go and see it.

4 My grandmother _____ a doctor when most doctors _____ men.

5 The children _____ very noisy yesterday. I hope they're quiet today.

6 The windows are open now, but they _____ this morning.

7 We _____ in bed until after 2 a.m. I'm really tired today!

8 My hair _____ brown when I _____ a baby. It's black now.

9 "_____ Lucy at the party?" "Yes, she _____."

10 "_____ you bored in the hospital?" "No, I _____. I read some good books."

2 Rewrite the sentences and questions in the simple past.

1 I am a taxi driver.
   I was a taxi driver.

2 He's not with us. He's at the shopping mall.
   _____

3 Those students aren't very friendly. They are unfriendly.
   _____

4 She's not at home. She's at the park.
   _____

5 "Are the pizzas cheap?" "Yes, they are."
   _____

6 "I'm not very happy." "I am!"
   _____

7 "Are your exams difficult?' "No, they're not."
   _____

8 "Is she your teacher?" "No, she's not."
   _____

9 Sam's not in class this week. He's on vacation.
   _____

10 "Is this question difficult to understand?" "No, it's not."
   _____

VOCABULARY: Celebrities

3 Match the celebrity words with a or b.

1 artist _____
2 athlete _____
3 DJ _____
4 movie director _____
5 soccer player _____
6 musician _____
7 racing driver _____
8 writer _____

a arts and entertainment
b sports

4 Complete the words for celebrities.

1 Most f __ __ __ __ __ __ m __ __ __ __ __ __ are young and beautiful.

2 P__ __ __ __ __ __ __ __ __ __ __ are public people, but they're not celebrities. They help people but aren't always famous.

3 He works for *The Daily Planet* newspaper and is an excellent j__ __ __ __ __ __ __ __ __.

4 Were the K__ __ __ and Q__ __ __ __ of Spain in London last week?

5 I love my work as a ballet d__ __ __ __ __, but the shows are difficult!

6 Now we can all be good p__ __ __ __ __ __ __ __ __ __ with a digital camera.

7 She wants to be a famous t__ __ __ __ __ p __ __ __ __ __ and win Wimbledon one day!

8 Do you find paintings by the Mexican a__ __ __ __ __ Diego Rivera interesting?

PRONUNCIATION: *was/were*

5 ▶ 7.1 Listen and repeat the questions and answers. Pay attention to the pronunciation of *was* and *were*.

1 A Where was he yesterday?
   B He was at home.

2 A Where were you on Friday?
   B I was at the post office.

3 A Where were they last week?
   B They were in Turkey.

4 A Where was your sister in June?
   B She was with my grandparents.

5 A Where was I on Saturday night?
   B You were at the club.

6 A Where were your parents in 1980?
   B They were in college.

SKILLS | 7B

LISTENING: Listening for dates

1 ▶7.2 Listen to the information. Match the celebrities with three of the words in the box.

| actor | dancer | king | musician | politician |
| queen | sports player | travel writer |

1 Ira Aldridge _____
2 Kumar Shri Ranjitsinhji _____
3 Isabella Bird _____

2 ▶7.2 Listen again. Complete the information about each person.

1 These three celebrities were famous in the _____ century.
2 Aldridge was in the UK from _____ until _____.
3 He was alive from July 24, 1807 until _____ _____.
4 Ranjitsinhji played for an English university team in the year _____.
5 His first national game for England was on _____ _____ _____.
6 Bird was _____ years old when she started traveling.
7 Her first book was in _____.
8 She was _____ years old when she was in Morocco.

3 ▶7.3 Listen and complete the sentences.

1 _____ _____ athlete.
2 The _____ is called "_____ _____ _____."
3 Before she _____ _____ artist, she _____ _____ _____ clerk.
4 My _____ _____ _____ _____ on Fridays and Saturdays.
5 He was born on _____ _____ -first, 1987.
6 The last time I _____ _____ a concert was _____ _____ in May.

4 Write the correct dates.

1 3/4 is ~~May~~ fourth.   _March_
2 8/15 is August fifth.   _____
3 4/10 is April second.   _____
4 1/2 is January twelfth.   _____
5 10/30 is November thirtieth.   _____
6 7/21 is June twenty-first.   _____
7 2/6 is February fifth.   _____
8 9/9 is September nineteenth. _____

7C LANGUAGE

GRAMMAR: Simple past: regular verbs

1 Order the words to make questions.

1 live / you / in the 2000s / did / where

_____?

2 did / listen to / music / you / then

_____?

3 was / your / favorite / singer / who

_____?

4 they / did / sing / what

_____?

5 an instrument / did / play / you

_____?

6 the name of / what / your band / was

_____?

2 Complete the sentences and questions. Use the verbs in parentheses in the simple past.

1 In South America, we _____ (visit) Colombia, Brazil and Peru.

2 "_____ (you/travel) to Berlin last year?" "Yes, I _____."

3 I _____ (not/watch) the game. Was it good?

4 She _____ (study) all day and all night before her final exam.

5 "_____ (he/arrive) at work on time this morning?" "No, _____. He was late again!"

6 After school they _____ (listen) to music.

7 We _____ (cook) chicken and vegetables for dinner yesterday.

8 "_____ (she/use) the remote control this morning?" "Yes, _____."

9 We _____ (not/like) the furniture in our hotel room.

10 The train trip was very long! The train _____ (stop) at lots of stations.

VOCABULARY: Time expressions

3 Which word does not make a time expression with the underlined word?

1 last month / morning / night / year

2 on six o'clock / February 10 / the weekend / April 18

3 in 1997 / the last decade / last year / the sixties

4 on 2004 / Wednesday / July 16 / Saturday

5 two fifteen / days / weeks / years ago

6 yesterday morning / afternoon / evening / night

7 on / last / in / this Monday

8 three weeks / a year / an hour / Wednesday ago

4 Complete the sentences with time expressions.

1 We worked until 2:00 a.m. last _____. We're very tired this morning!

2 When did I lose my passport? About 24 hours ago, so _____ afternoon.

3 She got her first job _____ 2012, and she works for the same company today.

4 Where was your summer vacation _____ year?

5 His computer stopped working _____ two o'clock this afternoon.

6 I met my girlfriend three months _____ at the bus stop!

7 They bought the GPS _____ Tuesday and now it doesn't work.

8 Did your mother and father meet in _____ 1980s?

9 My birthday is _____ January 24.

10 Did they go bike riding _____ the weekend?

PRONUNCIATION: -ed endings

5 ▶ 7.4 Complete each story 1–3 with three sentences a–i. For each story, choose only sentences where the -ed endings of the verbs in bold are pronounced the same (/d/, /t/, or /ɪd/). Then listen, check, and repeat.

1 Debbie **loved** trains when she was a student.
_b_ ___ ___

2 Edwina **needed** to go to the shopping mall.
___ ___ ___

3 Tina **watched** a movie in the afternoon.
___ ___ ___

a Then, in the evening, she **cooked** dinner.

b In 2017, she **traveled** to Boston.

c She **wanted** to buy a present for her boyfriend.

d She **tried** to win, but her friend was very good.

e But she was sad, so she **walked** to a club.

f She met a friend there and they **played** tennis.

g But everything was expensive and it **started** to rain.

h She **danced** all night there with her friends.

i She **visited** her brother, instead.

42

SKILLS 7D

WRITING: Writing informal e-mails

1 Read the e-mail. Then number the sentences 1–5.

Hi Geeta,

How are you? I hope the family is all well.

I'm in the UK! I wanted to tell you about my trip to Ramsgate with my friends from class on Saturday. It was fantastic! We started early and traveled by train. We arrived at ten o'clock. First, we visited a museum and listened to an interesting tour guide talk about the history of Ramsgate. Then we ate fish and chips in an old pub. After that, we walked around Ramsgate, but we were tired, so we stopped on the beach and had ice cream. It was a traditional day at the English seaside!

Please tell me your news. Did you do anything special on the weekend?

Take care,
Mishiko

a They sat next to the ocean. ____
b They arrived in Ramsgate. ____
c They learned about the town's past. ____
d They looked at the town. ____
e They had lunch. ____

2 Choose the correct options to complete 1–7.

1_____ James,
How are 2_____?
I hope 3_____ are well.
Did I 4_____ you about my vacation? We went to Marrakech in Morocco. It's an amazing place! Here's a photo of me in the local market.
Take 5_____ and 6_____ you soon!
Bye for 7_____,
Tracey

1	a Bye	b See	c Hi
2	a well	b things	c they
3	a things	b you	c it
4	a tell	b ask	c want
5	a soon	b care	c well
6	a see	b are	c hope
7	a well	b you	c now

3 Number the pictures 1–3. Then complete the sentences with the verbs in parentheses.

1 Nora arrived home at seven thirty.
First, _____ (listen).
Then _____ (cook).
After that, _____ (work) in her office.

2 Gavin had a very busy day.
First, _____ (help) his mom.
Then _____ (play) soccer.
After that, _____ (visit) his aunt.

4 Reply to Mishiko's e-mail. Tell her what you did last weekend. Make sure you:

- start and end your e-mail in a friendly way.
- use sequencers to show the order of events.

43

7 REVIEW and PRACTICE

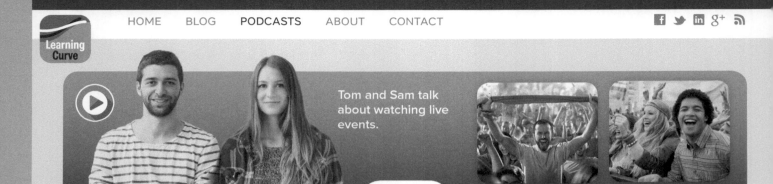

LISTENING

1 ▶ 7.5 Listen to the podcast about live events. Check (✔) the correct box for each person.

	Live	TV
Speaker 1 prefers		
Speaker 2 prefers		
Speaker 3 prefers		
Speaker 4 prefers		
Tom prefers		
Sam prefers		

2 ▶ 7.5 Listen again. Complete the sentences with one word from the podcast.

1 The survey said that _____ people prefer live events to TV.
2 Speaker 1 _____ watches soccer on TV.
3 He likes singing songs with his _____.
4 The weather at the _____ festival wasn't good.
5 Speaker 2 and her friends danced for _____.
6 Speaker 3 says the _____ was boring.
7 She can see the _____ better on TV.
8 Speaker 4 likes looking at _____ in art galleries.
9 He went to a gallery a few _____ ago.
10 Sam says that Tom is _____ because he prefers TV to live events.

READING

1 Read Simon's blog about celebrities. Match the celebrities with their jobs in photos a–d.

1 Hugh Jackman ____
2 Lady Gaga ____
3 Kanye West ____
4 Jennifer Hudson ____

2 Read the blog again. Write T (true), F (false), or NG (not given) if there is no information in the blog.

1 Hugh Jackman was in eight *X-Men* movies. ____
2 He lived in England for twelve months. ____
3 Lady Gaga helps other people. ____
4 She worked as a waitress to pay for school. ____
5 Kanye West didn't like working in the store. ____
6 His parents paid for all his clothes. ____
7 His company's clothes are expensive. ____
8 *Dreamgirls* is a movie about a restaurant. ____
9 Jennifer Hudson was born in Chicago. ____
10 She pays for her burgers at Burger King. ____

3 Order the letters to make celebrity jobs.

1 i v e o m   t i r e d r o c   m_____ d_____
2 c a r n i g   r i d r e v   r_____ d_____
3 o c s e c r   y p a e r l   s_____ p_____
4 h e a l t e t   a_____
5 n o i s h a f   d o l e m   f_____ m_____
6 n e t s i n   r e y a l p   t_____ p_____
7 t e r r i w   w_____
8 s m i n c i u a   m_____

REVIEW and PRACTICE 7

HOME **BLOG** PODCASTS ABOUT CONTACT

Our guest blogger Simon tells us what some stars of music and movies did in the past.

Before they were STARS

Most celebrities spend their days doing really cool and exciting things. But their lives weren't always so interesting. In fact, some celebrities had very normal jobs before they were famous.

In 2000, **Hugh Jackman** played the part of Wolverine in *X-Men*. The movie was very successful, and he was the star of eight more X-Movies in the 2000s and the 2010s. But Hugh had other jobs before he was an actor. When he was only eighteen he moved to England from Australia. He was a teacher in a very expensive school. His students liked him very much, but after a year he moved back to Australia.

a

These days everyone knows **Lady Gaga** for her music, her amazing shows, and her interesting clothes. She sells millions of records and she works for a lot of charities. On December 11, 2015, people chose her as the "Woman of the Year, 2015". But before she was famous, when she was in school, she worked as a waitress near her home in New York. She says she wanted the money to buy an expensive purse!

b

c

When **Kanye West** was a teenager, he worked in a clothing store. He liked the clothes, but he didn't enjoy the job. And he didn't make much money. In fact, he didn't earn enough money to buy the clothes in the store! Today he is one of the most famous musicians in the world and makes millions and millions of dollars. In 2015, his company started selling clothes. And they're not cheap!

d

Jennifer Hudson is a very famous actress and singer. She was the star of the movie *Dreamgirls* in 2006. But her first job was at a Burger King restaurant in Chicago. She started work in the restaurant when she was sixteen. Everyone says she liked to sing a lot at work! In 2007, Burger King called Jennifer to say she never needs to pay for food – she gets free food for life!

45

UNIT 8

Travel

8A LANGUAGE

GRAMMAR: Simple past: irregular verbs

1 Write the simple past verbs.

1. We h_____ a loud noise from the street.
2. Karen s_____ her money on clothes.
3. No one k_____ the answer to her question.
4. Who t_____ you English last year?
5. Brendan f_____ a wallet on the bus.
6. Sue w_____ a letter to her grandmother.
7. They b_____ some vegetables at the market.
8. He c_____ a new lamp for his office.

2 Complete the sentences with the simple past verbs.

Across

1. This shirt only _____ me $20 at the shopping mall.
3. She _____ her house keys in her purse.
5. I _____ my boyfriend in college in 2016.
6. They _____ to Cartagena in an old car.
7. He _____ me a book to read.
8. It _____ three days to paint our new house.

Down

1. I _____ to work early yesterday.
2. Her cat _____ next to her on the sofa.
4. Hi! I _____ you were on vacation this week – why are you at work?
6. We _____ housework, and then went to bed early.

VOCABULARY: Travel verbs

3 Choose one option in each sentence which is not correct.

1. He *got in / got on / took* a taxi to the station.
2. Do you know how to ride a *bike / horse / car*?
3. I don't want to miss my *bike / bus / train* tomorrow!
4. Let's take *a taxi / a bus / a car* to the hospital.
5. They *flew / got off / sailed* from Panamá to Colombia.
6. We can book our *flight / hotel / subway* on the Internet.
7. Where do we *walk / get off / take* the train?
8. They *got off / got on / got lost* the bus at the grocery store.

4 Complete the sentences with travel verbs.

1. _____ the car, please. We need to leave now!
2. Can I _____ the flight online now, or do I need my passport?
3. I _____ the train to work. It gives me time to read and relax.
4. If you _____ the bus you need to wait for the next one.
5. Is it OK if we _____ to the park? It's a lovely evening and I don't have a bike.
6. You don't want to _____, so take a good map.
7. Most people prefer to _____ long distances because planes are fast.
8. She can't _____ her motorcycle to work this week because her brother has it.
9. The ferry doesn't _____ when there is bad weather.
10. To go to the museum, take the subway and _____ at the third station.

PRONUNCIATION: Irregular simple past verbs

5 ▶ 8.1 Choose the correct sound for the verbs in each sentence. Then listen, check, and repeat.

1 Bob got on the train at 6 a.m.	/ɑ/	/ɔ/	/ow/
2 Do you know he rode home?	/ɑ/	/ɔ/	/ow/
3 He walked to town and saw his friends.	/ɑ/	/ɔ/	/ow/
4 I thought I saw a tour guide.	/ɑ/	/ɔ/	/ow/
5 She drove to Rome.	/ɑ/	/ɔ/	/ow/
6 Paul lost his ticket.	/ɑ/	/ɔ/	/ow/
7 They chose a cheap hotel.	/ɑ/	/ɔ/	/ow/

SKILLS 8B

READING: Understanding the main idea

1 Write the words for weather and seasons.

1 It's w_____ and cl_____ today.
2 It's s_____ in Canada.
3 In Chicago, it's r_____ now.
4 In the mornings, it's often f_____, but by lunchtime, it's nearly always s_____.
5 F_____ and s_____ are good seasons to visit southern Europe.
6 When it's s_____ in North America, it's w_____ in South America.

2 Look at the title and the photos. Read the first sentences of each paragraph. Which question does the article answer?

a Why do we travel to places with warm weather?
b Why do people go to places with bad weather?
c Which countries have hot, cold, and windy weather?

3 Read the whole article and choose the correct options.

1 The Marathon des Sables runners do the event in
  a hot weather b cold weather c hot and cold weather.
2 Mauro Prosperi got lost because
  a it was very hot b the weather was bad
  c he didn't have any water.
3 Scott's team went to Cape Crozier because
  a they wanted to be the first people there.
  b their friends were there.
  c they wanted to find something.
4 During the Antarctic trip, the men didn't see
  a the sun. b many penguins. c any other people.
5 Windsurfers at the Défi races
  a come from many different countries.
  b sometimes travel at 144 kilometers an hour.
  c are all French.
6 The windsurfing speed record was in
  a France. b Namibia. c Gruissan.

4 Complete the sentences with the correct option.

1 It is *not very / pretty* foggy today – I can see the top of those hills.
2 Don't drink that coffee! It's *not very / really* hot! Wait a few minutes.
3 I don't want to read the rest of this book. It's *not very / pretty* good.
4 I'm *not very / really* surprised you are here. I thought you were in Brazil.
5 It was *not very / pretty* cold this morning. I needed a sweater when I wasn't in the sun.
6 That wasn't a good horror movie last night. I was *pretty / not very* scared at all!
7 Our exam was *pretty / really* easy. Some questions were difficult, but I'm sure I passed.
8 You got three pizzas for only $12? That's *not very / really* cheap!

Usually, when we travel, we go to places where the weather is warm and sunny. We don't like it when it's very hot, cold, windy, or foggy. But some people look for extreme weather. Are they crazy? You decide!

A **The Marathon des Sables is a six-day, 200-kilometer trek through the Sahara desert in southern Morocco.** Runners carry everything they need with them, including water. It can reach 50°C, but at night, they often sleep in temperatures below 0°! In 1994, Italian athlete Mauro Prosperi got lost for nine days after a sand storm. He ran 299 kilometers in the wrong direction … into Algeria!

B **In July 1911, three members of Scott's team to the Antarctic traveled to a place called Cape Crozier.** The men walked for 19 days in the 24-hour darkness of the Antarctic winter. They carried their food and tent behind them. It was sometimes –70°C. Why? They went to collect penguin eggs!

C **Every year, more than a thousand windsurfers from 40 countries go to Gruissan in southern France for the Défi Wind races.** This is an excellent place for windsurfing because it's very windy, with winds sometimes reaching 144 kilometers an hour. But Antoine Albeau holds the windsurfing speed record. He was in Namibia when he traveled at 98 kilometers an hour on November 2nd, 2015.

8C LANGUAGE

GRAMMAR: there was/were

1 Match the two parts of the sentences.

1 At the party, there was some ____
2 There was a ____
3 There was ____
4 There were ____
5 There were lots ____
6 There weren't ____
7 Was there ____
8 Were there ____

a a photographer? Yes, there was!
b no singer.
c any celebrities? No, there weren't.
d any waiters or waitresses.
e DJ all evening.
f of friendly people.
g great music.
h some sandwiches and cakes.

2 Complete the dialogue with *there was/were* in the correct form.

Pablo	Grandfather, ¹_____ any stores here in 1950?
Grandfather	Oh, yes, ²_____ lots of stores, but ³_____ only one shopping mall, and it was small.
Pablo	And what about places to eat?
Grandfather	Well, ⁴_____ some cafés, but ⁵_____ any pizza restaurants or places like that.
Pablo	⁶_____ a swimming pool?
Grandfather	No, ⁷_____. But ⁸_____ a park if you wanted to go for a walk.
Pablo	And what about transportation? ⁹_____ a train station?
Grandfather	Yes, ¹⁰_____. It was very important, because ¹¹_____ many cars in those days.
Pablo	And what did you do in the evenings?
Grandfather	Well, ¹²_____ no club for young people like there is today.
Pablo	That sounds boring!

VOCABULARY: Nature

3 ▶ 8.2 Complete each sentence with the words in the box. Then decide which picture each sentence describes. Listen and check.

| grass | river | ocean | sky | sun | trees |

1 You can see it's windy today. Look at the _____!   a   b
2 There are some beautiful _____ above the water.   a   b
3 The evening _____ is very clear today.   a   b
4 The _____ next to the water looks very soft.   a   b
5 I don't think the water goes very fast along this _____.   a   b
6 You can still see the _____, but not for much longer.   a   b

 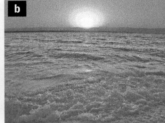

4 Complete the nature words.

1 I can see a large black c_ _ _ _ in the sky.
2 My dog loves to play in the f_ _ _ _ next to our apartment.
3 Those f_ _ _ _ _ _ are all different colors: red, yellow, and pink.
4 It's summer, but it's not hot up here on the m_ _ _ _ _ _ _.
5 We had lunch on the b_ _ _ _, but it was pretty hot.
6 There are more than twenty types of trees in this f_ _ _ _ _.

PRONUNCIATION: Sentence stress

5 ▶ 8.3 Underline the stressed words. Then listen, check, and repeat.

1 "Was there a television in your room?" "No, there wasn't."
2 "Was there an evening meal?" "Yes, there was."
3 "Were there any clubs?" "Yes, there were."
4 "Were there good restaurants?" "No, there weren't."
5 "Was there any music?" "Yes, there was."
6 "Were there many nice people?" "No, there weren't!"
7 "Were there any stores?" "Yes, there were."
8 "Was there a swimming pool?" "No, there wasn't."

SKILLS 8D

SPEAKING: Buying a ticket

1 ▶ 8.4 Listen to two telephone conversations. Find one mistake in A and one mistake in B and write the correct information.

1 Conversation 1: _____
2 Conversation 2: _____

A

B

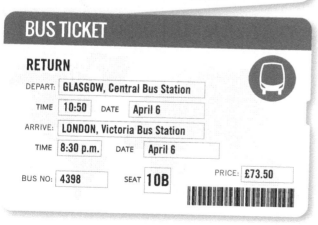

2 ▶ 8.4 Listen again. Number the phrases 1–8 in the order you hear them.

a I'd like a ticket to Glasgow, please. ____
b When do you want to travel? ____
c Would you like a one-way or round-trip ticket? ____
d What time does the flight leave? ____
e How much is it? ____
f I'd like a one-way ticket to Brazil, please. ____
g When does it arrive? ____
h What kind of ticket would you like? ____

3 ▶ 8.5 Order the words to make sentences and questions. Then listen and check.

1 a / Brisbane / I'd / like / round-trip / ticket / to
   _____.

2 does / it / time / leave / what
   _____?

3 arrive / does / in / London / it / when
   _____?

4 a / like / you / one-way / or / round-trip / ticket / would
   _____?

5 $8.90 / a / for / it's / one-way / ticket
   _____

6 do / return / to / want / when / you
   _____?

4 ▶ 8.6 Listen and complete the conversations.

1 A _____, FPQ Couriers. _____ _____ Hanif speaking. How can I help you?
  B Good _____. I'd like to speak to Mr. Travers, please.
  A Who's calling?
  B _____ _____ _____ Diane Godridge.
  ~
  C Thanks for _____, Ms. Godridge. Goodbye.
  B _____.

2 A Good _____. Jessica _____.
  B Hello. _____ _____ William Sharp from Oldham Print Services. Is Karen there, please?
  ~
  C Thanks for _____ _____, William.
  B Thank you, Karen. _____ for now.

49

8 REVIEW and PRACTICE

Tom and Sam talk about Cornelia's difficult trip.

LISTENING

1 ▶ 8.7 Listen to the podcast about a bad trip. Number the things that happened (a–h) in the correct order (1–8).

- a Cornelia took a taxi. ___
- b She asked a woman for help. ___
- c She used the Internet. ___
- d She went to a café. ___
- e She ran very fast. ___
- f She got an e-mail. ___
- g She fell over. ___
- h She asked a man for help. ___

2 ▶ 8.7 Listen again. Choose the correct answers.

1 Cornelia got ___ about the interview.
   a a letter   b an e-mail   c a phone call
2 Cornelia's interview was ___ miles from her home.
   a 300   b 200   c 100
3 She didn't fly because there weren't any ___ flights.
   a early   b cheap   c quick
4 She didn't know the ___ of her interview.
   a time   b address   c date
5 She took a ___ home from the station.
   a bus   b train   c taxi
6 The train was very ___.
   a fast   b expensive   c slow
7 At the station, she asked a ___ for directions.
   a man   b woman   c tourist
8 There were only ___ minutes before the interview.
   a five   b fifteen   c 50
9 Cornelia had her interview in ___.
   a an office   b a store   c a café
10 Cornelia didn't get ___.
   a the job   b a coffee   c an interview

READING

1 Read Marc's blog about South Korea. Match paragraphs 1–4 with photos a–d.

1 ___
2 ___
3 ___
4 ___

2 Read the blog again. Write Y (yes), N (no), or DS (doesn't say) if there is no information in the blog.

1 Marc thinks Korea is horrible in the summer. ___
2 A lot of people go to Imjado beach. ___
3 The weather in the fall is always warm. ___
4 Marc thinks fall is the best time to visit Seoul forest. ___
5 It snows all over South Korea. ___
6 There are many mountains in Korea. ___
7 You can't ski near Seoul. ___
8 Spring is everyone's favorite season in South Korea. ___
9 Marc doesn't like cherry blossoms. ___
10 Koreans often travel along the river by bike. ___

REVIEW and PRACTICE 8

HOME **BLOG** PODCASTS ABOUT CONTACT

This week's guest blogger Marc tells us why his parents' home country is a great place to visit at all times of the year.

SOUTH KOREA
a country for all seasons!

1 Summer (June to August)

When I was young, people always said to me, "Don't come to Korea in summer – it's horrible!" It's true that it is very hot, but this is a good reason to go to the beach! The most famous beach is Haeundae near the city of Busan. It is very popular in the summer, with thousands of people enjoying the sun. In fact, sometimes it's not very nice because of all the people. So try the island of Imjado for its quiet beach and beautiful ocean.

2 Fall (September to November)

The weather in the fall starts pretty warm, but by the end of the season it's cold. If you are in the capital city, I recommend a visit to the Seoul Forest. It's a very big park downtown with more than 400,000 trees. Fall is the perfect time to visit because the leaves on the trees are all different colors. It's beautiful!

3 Winter (December to February)

South Korea in winter is very cold and windy, and it snows a lot in the north of the country, but there are still fun things to do. Remember that it has a lot of mountains, so it's easy to find a place to ski. The best places to ski are in the east of the country, but that's not the only place. You can even go on a skiing day-trip from Seoul. Then go to a concert or music festival in the evening. There is a lot of live music in Seoul.

4 Spring (March to May)

After the cold (and sometimes difficult) winter, people are always happy at the start of spring. It often seems like everybody is out looking at the new flowers! South Korea is famous for its cherry blossoms – I think they are the most beautiful flowers in the world! When they're not looking at flowers, people often spend spring days bike riding along the Han river. It's a long river with large areas of grass on either side. It's a very good way to get some sun on your face!

UNIT 9 Shopping

9A LANGUAGE

GRAMMAR: Present continuous

1 Choose the correct options to complete the sentences.

1 What's Vicky *made / makes / making* in the kitchen right now?
2 Mia and Lucas *are / do / is* helping their brother with his new phone.
3 "Are you reading to Emily?" "Yes, I *am / do / reading*. It's her favorite book."
4 I'm not *use / uses / using* my bike this week.
5 Gloria and I *aren't / don't / 's not* talking to each other these days.
6 *Am / Are / Is* you and your friends getting ready to go out right now?
7 "Are Luka and Ibrahim playing basketball?" "No they *'re not / don't / 's not*. It's handball."
8 Adam *am / 're not / 's not* working in the office today.
9 Rebecca's *watched / watches / watching* soccer with her friends right now.
10 "Are we going to the grocery store?" "Yes, we *am / are / go*."

2 Complete the sentences with the correct form of the verbs in parentheses.

1 A What _____ right now? (do)
  B I'm on the bus. _____ to school. (go)
2 A _____ at a hotel this week? (stay)
  B No, we _____. We're in our tent. It's cold!
3 A I can hear another person with you. Who _____ to? (talk)
  B That's my grandmother. _____ her today. (visit)
4 A _____ in the competition? (sing)
  B Yes, they _____. They're on stage right now.
5 A _____ Dad _____ lunch ready? (get)
  B No, he _____ cookies. I love his cooking! (make)
6 A What _____ in the bathroom? (do)
  B She _____ a shower. (take)
7 A _____ to California today? (drive)
  B Yes, but we _____ at a restaurant now. The driver needs to take a break. (stop)
8 A _____ anyone _____ here right now? (sit)
  B No, that seat's free. And I _____ now, so you can have both seats! (leave)

VOCABULARY: Clothes

3 Complete the clothes words.

1 I like these s_____ and s_____ – they look good on my big feet!
2 It's snowing. Put a c_____ and h_____ on!
3 She wore a long red d_____ and a pair of beautiful brown b_____.
4 This s_____ keeps me warm in winter.
5 These p_____ are very big. I need a b_____ to make them stay up.
6 On weekends, I wear my old pair of blue j_____ and T-_____ with my favorite bands on them.

4 Look at the pictures and complete the crossword.

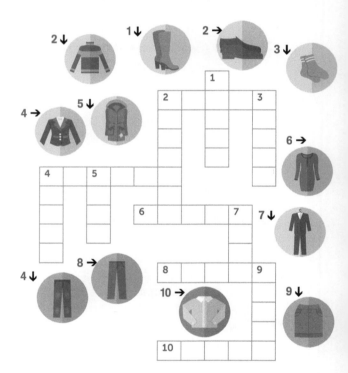

PRONUNCIATION: -ing endings

5 ▶ 9.1 Listen and repeat. Pay attention to the /ŋ/ sound.

1 Why are you going out?
2 Who's helping me do housework?
3 I'm staying on my own.
4 I think she's speaking in Swahili.
5 We're just arriving now.
6 They're not looking after the house very well.

52

SKILLS 9B

LISTENING: Identifying key points

1 ▶ 9.2 Listen to the podcast about the meanings of colors. Match the colors with the feelings.

1 in love   _____   a black
2 angry   _____ _____   b blue
3 calm   _____ _____ _____ c green
4 sad   _____ _____ _____ d red
5 scared   _____   e white
                                f yellow

2 ▶ 9.2 Read these sentences from the podcast. Match them with a or b. Listen again and check.

1 So once again, colors change their meaning in different countries.   _____   a emphasizing or repeating
2 Red hearts and red flowers show people that you love them.   _____   b giving examples or more information
3 The reason for this is that when we are angry our faces are red.   _____
4 Not just different – totally different!   _____

3 ▶ 9.3 Listen to six sentences. Write the filler word (*uh*, *so*, *um*, or *well*) that you hear.

1 _____   4 _____
2 _____   5 _____
3 _____   6 _____

4 Complete the conversations with the correct adjectives.

1 angry / surprised
  A Please don't be _____. I used all your milk.
    I'm sorry.
  B I'm just a little _____ because you don't
    drink milk!

2 excited / worried
  A Are you _____ about starting a new school?
  B Yes, I am. I'm happy, but I'm a little _____,
    too. I hope the other students aren't unfriendly!

3 thirsty / hungry
  A Are you feeling _____? Do you want a
    sandwich?
  B No, but I am a bit _____. Can I have some
    juice?

4 calm / scared
  A My sister is _____ by movies like *Dracula*
    and *Frankenstein*.
  B They certainly don't make me feel _____!

5 happy / tired
  A Your brother doesn't look _____. Is he OK?
  B He's fine, but he's pretty _____. It was a long
    day at work.

6 bored / sad
  A I'm not _____ that I didn't stay at the party. It
    was noisy, and the food wasn't good.
  B You did the right thing. I stayed and I was really
    _____!

53

9C LANGUAGE

GRAMMAR: *How often* + expressions of frequency

1 Number the frequency expressions 1–10, from the least often to the most often.

a every month ___
b every week ___
c every year ___
d four times a year ___
e never _1_
f once a day ___
g twice a day ___
h twice a week ___
i twice a year ___
j two or three times a month ___

2 Order the words to make sentences and questions.

1 A does / her family / how / Lupita / often / visit

_____?

B a / goes / she / twice / usually / year

_____.

2 A every / exercise / he / week / does

_____?

B a / goes / the gym / he / month / once / to

_____.

3 A a / a / haircut / have / I / twice / year

_____.

B not / often / that's / very

_____!

4 A do / how / their parents / see / often / they

_____?

B times / three / month / them / they / a / visit

_____.

5 A check / day / do / your e-mails / every / you

_____?

B a / day / four / I / check / or / three / times / them

_____.

6 A always / does / go out / on / Saturdays / she

_____?

B a / goes / month / once / or / she / out / twice

_____.

VOCABULARY: Shopping

3 ▶ 9.4 Number the sentences 1–9 in the correct order to make a paragraph. Then listen and check.

a I usually shop at the market. It's friendly, but you have to pay with ... _1_

b ... credit card at the shopping ... ___

c ... cash there. You can pay by ... ___

d ... mall. For presents, I sometimes go to the department ... ___

e ... money at local ... ___

f ... on. I want to start selling things online soon! ___

g ... online for books and clothes, but not for shoes – you can't try them ... ___

h ... stores. A few years ago I started shopping ... ___

i ... store, but it's expensive. I prefer to spend my ... ___

4 Complete the shopping words.

1 Do you want to g_____ s_____? Let's go now, before the s_____ m_____ closes.

2 At the m_____ you can b_____ meat, fish, fruit, and vegetables.

3 This is a d_____ s_____, so why can't I p_____ b_____ credit card?

4 It's easy to s_____ lots of m_____ with just one click when you shop o_____.

5 She makes clothes and she s_____ them in a few of the l_____ s_____ in her town.

6 If you know your size, sometimes you don't need to t_____ o_____ new clothes.

7 You can only pay w_____ c_____ here. We don't have a credit card machine.

PRONUNCIATION: Sentence stress

5 ▶ 9.5 Underline the stressed words. Then listen, check, and repeat.

1 He goes swimming twice a week.
2 They watch movies two or three times a month.
3 I finish a book about once a week.
4 We take a vacation in Thailand every year.
5 Do you drive every day?
6 She takes a shower once or twice a day.

54

SKILLS 9D

WRITING: Describing a photo

1 Look at the photo and read the e-mail. Find three differences between them.

> Hi Chloe,
>
> How are things? I hope you're well.
>
> I had a great time in London last weekend. I went with four of my friends from college. We took the bus and got there early. First we went to a museum, and then we went shopping.
>
> Here's a photo of us on the street. We're carrying a lot of shopping! There are only three people in the photo because Karol is taking the photo. That's me on the left. Look! I'm wearing the black hat you bought for me. The friend at the top in a T-shirt is David. Paula and Alex are standing next to me.
>
> E-mail me soon, please. I want to know how the concert was.
>
> Izzie

2 Find one mistake in each sentence and write the correct words.

1 There are a window on the right of the photo. _____
2 They are four people in the photo. _____
3 They look in a window. _____
4 David is standing to the top. _____
5 The man in the left is Alex. _____
6 The other woman on the middle is Paula. _____

3 Look at the picture and write sentences.

1 That / our mother / middle
   _____.

2 My little sister Sofia / top of the photo
   _____.

3 She / sit / on my dad's shoulders
   _____.

4 David / middle, next / Mom
   _____.

5 There / leaves and grass / bottom
   _____.

6 And that's me / right
   _____.

4 Choose a photo of you with your family or friends. Write an e-mail to a friend and describe it. Make sure you:
   • explain who the people are and their position in the photo.
   • use the present continuous to say what they are doing.
   • use *there is/are* to say what things are in the photo.

55

9 REVIEW and PRACTICE

HOME   BLOG   PODCASTS   ABOUT   CONTACT

Tom and Sam talk about shopping.

LISTENING

1 ▶9.6 Listen to the podcast about clothes and shopping. Number the clothes 1–10 in the order you hear them.

a boots ____
b coat ____
c dress ____
d hat ____
e jeans ____
f sweater ____
g shirt ____
h shoes ____
i skirt ____
j pants ____

2 ▶9.6 Listen to the podcast about clothes and shopping. How often do the speakers go shopping? Complete the sentences.

1 Speaker 1: every _____
2 Speaker 2: _____ times a week
3 Speaker 3: three times a _____
4 Speaker 4: every _____

3 ▶9.6 Listen again. Complete the sentences with one or two words.

1 Tom often wears the same _____.
2 Yesterday, Sam and Tom went to Greenway _____.
3 Speaker 1 is buying a _____ and _____.
4 Speaker 1 is paying by _____.
5 Speaker 2 is trying on _____.
6 Speaker 2 always shops _____.
7 Speaker 3 thinks the _____ is horrible.
8 Speaker 3 is meeting her _____.
9 Speaker 4 thinks the _____ has too many colors.
10 Speaker 4 thinks the _____ is beautiful.

READING

1 Read Simon's blog about emojis. Choose the best summary.

a Emojis give people problems.
b Everyone loves emojis because they are quick.
c Simon's friends like emojis.

2 Read the blog again. Choose the correct answers to complete the sentences.

1 Simon's friends ____ send him emojis.
   a sometimes
   b often
   c never

2 He says people ____ a new language with emojis.
   a can learn
   b don't need to learn
   c are speaking

3 He didn't send his sister a message because he was ____.
   a busy
   b surprised
   c angry

4 The message from his friend made him ____.
   a worried
   b bored
   c sad

5 His girlfriend didn't reply because he didn't ____.
   a use the right emoji
   b reply to her message
   c feel excited

6 He doesn't like emojis because ____.
   a they're boring
   b there are too many
   c they can cause problems

56

REVIEW and PRACTICE 9

HOME   **BLOG**   PODCASTS   ABOUT   CONTACT

Guest blogger Simon writes about the little pictures we send on our phones.

Emoji problems

I hate emojis

There – I said it! My friends send me funny pictures every day, but I don't like them. Do you want to know why? OK, but first let's look at why emojis are so popular.

First, they are quick. We live in a fast, busy world, and it only takes a second to send an emoji. Next, they are international. American, Brazilian, Chinese – we can all send and understand messages. And we don't need to learn a new language! And finally, a lot of people think emojis are fun. They make people laugh!

But emojis aren't always good. In fact, they often give me problems. Here are three stories from my life to show you what I mean!

Last year, my sister had an interview for a very good job. She sent me this message: "I got the job!" I was busy and I didn't have time to send her a message. So I sent a "surprised" emoji. She replied with an "angry" emoji. I didn't understand, so I called her later. She asked why I sent her a "surprised" face. "You think I'm not good enough for the job!" she said. But it wasn't true!

An old friend sent me a message with some sad news. I tried to send a "sad" face emoji to him, but I was tired and I didn't have my glasses. And I sent him a "bored" face! The next morning I saw my message and I was really worried! I called my friend and said I was sorry, but everything was OK.

My girlfriend and I went on vacation last year. The night before we flew, she sent me a message. It was a plane, a heart, and a happy face. I tried to reply with an "excited" face, but I did it wrong. I sent her a "scared" face. She didn't reply!

So that is why I don't like emojis. But sometimes I think everyone else loves them! Here are some interesting emoji facts. Did you know …

- the first emoji was in 1999. A Japanese man called Shigetaka Kurita made it.
- July 17 is World Emoji Day. They chose that date because it is the date you can see on the emoji of a calendar.
- the world sends more than five billion emojis every day.
- the most popular emoji last year was the crying and laughing face. Second was the kissing emoji. And third was the red heart.

UNIT 10

Time out

10A — LANGUAGE

GRAMMAR: Present continuous for future plans

1 Order the words to complete the conversation.

A ¹ this weekend / you / doing / what / are?

B ² my grandfather / am / looking after / I. What about you? ³ you / tomorrow / are / studying?

A ⁴ I / am / yes. ⁵ going out / are / on Sunday / you? ⁶ practicing for / we / our concert / are.

B That sounds great!

A ⁷ there / after lunch / is / Patricia / driving. Do you and Tom want to come with us?

B Yes, please. ⁸ in the morning / going / we / swimming / are. You can meet us at the pool!

1 _____?
2 _____.
3 _____?
4 _____.
5 _____?
6 _____.
7 _____.
8 _____.

2 Complete the sentences with the correct pairs of verbs in the present continuous.

| write/finish | do/go | fly/see | help/cook |
| meet/take | not sail/drive | run/plan | visit/have |

1 I _____ to Brazil on Monday, but I _____ my grandparents there until Friday.

2 We _____ friends tomorrow morning in Rio. We _____ lunch at a restaurant together.

3 _____ you _____ anything tonight? Francine and I _____ to the movies.

4 My sister _____ in the race next month. She _____ to run every day before then!

5 They _____ to Greece tomorrow on their boat. They _____ there, instead.

6 _____ Harry _____ his mother at the airport this evening or _____ she _____ the bus?

7 When _____ he _____ his next book? I _____ this one today.

8 I _____ Izzie buy a new tablet tomorrow, and then she _____ dinner for me.

VOCABULARY: Free-time activities

3 Choose one option in each sentence which is <u>not</u> correct.

1 Are they having a *video / barbecue / good time*?

2 I'm not staying at a *friend's house / tent / hotel*.

3 Please, can we visit *the museum / my parents / a hotel*?

4 Can I watch *a video / the soccer game / museum*?

5 We had the *art gallery / barbecue / party* in our backyard.

6 Let's go to *a festival / a video / the beach*!

4 What are the people going to do? Complete the sentences.

1 I'm ready to relax in front of the TV. I'm w*atching* ___*a*___ m_*ovie*___.

2 Malachi loves history and old objects. He is going downtown. He's v_____ _____ m_____.

3 My parents are seeing their favorite musician. They're g_____ _____ _____ c_____.

4 Paola is tired after work. She wants to take a bath and go to bed early. She's s_____ h_____.

5 He enjoys looking at paintings and photographs. He is v_____ _____ a_____ g_____.

6 We're cooking in the backyard today. We're h_____ _____ b_____.

7 Alice enjoys being outside and seeing her favorite bands. This weekend she's g_____ _____ _____ f_____.

PRONUNCIATION: Sentence stress

5 ▶10.1 Listen and repeat. Underline the stressed words.

1 **A** Who is she seeing tonight?
   B She's meeting her friends from college.

2 **A** Are they watching a movie?
   B No, they're not. They're watching soccer.

3 **A** I'm visiting a friend in Miami.
   B Are you taking the bus?

4 **A** Is he staying at home this evening?
   B Yes, he is. He's doing housework.

5 **A** Which beach are you going to?
   B We're talking about that now.

6 **A** How are we getting there?
   B We're taking the train.

58

SKILLS 10B

READING: Scanning for information

1 Quickly read the guide. Match events 1–7 with A–E. There are two extra events.

1 a movie _____
2 a jazz concert _____
3 a classical concert _____
4 a rock concert _____
5 a festival _____
6 a talk _____
7 an art exhibition _____

2 Underline the key words in each question. Then scan the text for the answers.

1 How many bands are playing on Friday? _____
2 Which event is only in the morning? _____
3 How many events are only free for students? _____
4 How old do you need to be to watch the movie? _____
5 What type of movie is at the movie theater this weekend? _____
6 How much is the art exhibition if you're not a student? _____
7 What time does the event at Cambalache start? _____
8 Which two places are on the same street? _____ _____

3 Complete each sentence with the affirmative or negative imperative of the verbs in the box. There are two extra verbs.

| be | book | buy | close | come |
| go | have | tell | wait | watch |

1 _____ a ticket for me at the station. I already have one.
2 Please _____ to the next class with your questions about the movie.
3 I'm working late tonight so _____ for me for dinner.
4 Flights are expensive, so _____ them very early!
5 See you after the party. And _____ a good time!
6 _____ the door. I like it open.
7 I'm putting my coat on now. _____ without me!
8 _____ him I have a present for him. It's a secret.

THIS WEEK'S main events in and around town

A

Battle of the bands FINAL
See the best rock music in town. Three local bands are playing to win the $500 prize – don't miss it!
Friday 16, 8 p.m.
Cellar 21, Cass St.
$12, Students $10

B

Music of the 20s, 30s and 40s
A look back at the jazz of New Orleans. With Charles Rayburn and Lolo Gonzalez and his band.
Cambalache bar, Fenton Street
Saturday 10 p.m. till late!
$15

C

Variplex Movie Theater
Police Force 2 - Action comedy (+12 years)
The second in the Police Force series – the first was exciting and funny!
**** The Daily Show, ****Movietime website
4:30 and 7:30 Sat. and Sun.
Tickets: $8.50 from movie theater box office

D

Talk: "From Dinosaur to Dodo"
Natural Science Museum
Wednesday 10:30–11:30 a.m.
Speakers include Margaret Pearson "TV's dinosaur expert." Come with questions!
Get tickets online before Wednesday for free.
School groups welcome! Find out more at www.NatSciMus.ed.us

E

Fenton gallery
"Down" is an exhibition of landscape paintings and sculptures by local artists. Starts this week for two weeks only.
Monday thru Friday 10–6, Fenton Street, admission $3 (free for students)

4 Order the letters to make words about music and movies. Then write them in the correct category.

| ~~coinat~~ | callsasic | mycoed | adarm | leecorntic | phi-pho |
| rorrho | zjaz | opp | cork | caronem | sceenic oftnic |

types of movie	types of music
action	_____
_____	_____
_____	_____

59

10C LANGUAGE

GRAMMAR: Question review

1 Order the words to make questions.

1 a museum / did / last visit / when / Fabien

_____?

2 did / the concert / like / he

_____?

3 do / go / how often / to / the movies / you

_____?

4 right now / can / bands / I / see / what

_____?

5 the festival / was / where

_____?

6 are / favorite / actors / who / your

_____?

7 DVD / it / can / on / watch / we

_____?

8 any / are / making / new movies / now / they

_____?

2 Match a–f with the questions in exercise 1.

a simple present _____

b simple present of *be* _____

c simple past _____ _____

d simple past of *be* _____

e present continuous _____

f with *can* _____ _____

3 Complete the questions with the verbs in parentheses in the correct tense.

1 _____ you _____ a good book right now? (read)

2 What type of games _____ she _____ playing when she was a child? (like)

3 Who _____ your favorite writer now? (be)

4 How often _____ you usually _____ each year? (fly)

5 How many people _____ at his last party? (be)

6 _____ there lots of grocery stores in your town these days? (be)

7 "_____ he _____ a musical instrument?" "No, he can't." (play)

8 When _____ you _____ shopping with your sister – next Saturday or Sunday? (go)

9 _____ Jean sometimes _____ to jazz? (listen)

10 _____ you _____ that horror movie last night? (see)

VOCABULARY: Sports and games

4 Choose the correct options to complete the sentences.

1 How often do you _____ running on the beach?
a play   b do   c go

2 I _____ gymnastics when I was a young girl.
a did   b played   c went

3 I told him I'm no good at chess, but he still wanted to _____ with me.
a go   b do   c play

4 He _____ yoga on weekends.
a does   b goes   c plays

5 Last weekend, they _____ rock climbing.
a played   b went   c did

6 She didn't study much in college. She mostly _____ videogames!
a did   b played   c went

7 They're _____ soccer in the park.
a going   b doing   c playing

8 We're _____ skiing soon. I'm so excited!
a doing   b playing   c going

5 Complete the sports or games words.

1 Does he play h_____ on grass or ice?

2 I did k_____ until I got my blue belt; I didn't get a black one!

3 A b_____ and a t_____ ball are pretty small!

4 Last winter, we went s_____ in the Atlantic Ocean. It was really cold!

5 Most professional b_____ players are more than 6.5 feet tall.

6 I'm doing p_____. It's a bit like yoga.

7 One popular sport people play on the beach is v_____.

8 This weekend, they're going h_____ in the hills while the weather is good.

9 Let's play t_____ tomorrow – with two more people we can play doubles.

10 He couldn't go b_____ yesterday because his bike is broken.

PRONUNCIATION: Intonation in questions

6 ▶10.2 Listen and repeat the questions. Pay attention to the intonation.

1 What's your hobby?

2 Are you doing it this weekend?

3 When did you start?

4 Was it difficult?

5 How often do you do it?

6 Is it expensive?

SKILLS 10D

SPEAKING: Asking about a tourist attraction

1 ▶10.3 Listen to the conversation. Number the photos in the order the people talk about these things (1–5).

a ___   b ___   c ___   d ___   e ___

2 ▶10.3 Listen again. Are the sentences true (T) or false (F)?

1 The tourist knows Valparaíso well. ___
2 She and her boyfriend are staying at a hotel. ___
3 She really wants to go to the Pablo Neruda museum. ___
4 The museum doesn't have a gift shop. ___
5 They want to go to the museum today. ___
6 On Saturday, there is an event at the museum. ___
7 They need to pay 2,500 pesos to get in. ___

3 ▶10.3 Read the sentences from the conversation. Which words did you hear in the questions? Listen again and check.

1 Is there a *café / gift shop*?
2 *When / Which days* is it open?
3 What time does it *close / open* today?
4 How do you *get there / pay*?
5 Are there any *concerts / special events* today?
6 What is there to do *if it rains / in the evening*?

4 ▶10.4 Listen to a conversation. Check (✓) the expressions you hear.

1 Did you enjoy your trip? ___
2 How was your trip? ___
3 Did you have fun? ___
4 Oh, OK. ___
5 Oh really? ___
6 Sounds fantastic! ___
7 Sounds wonderful! ___
8 That sounds interesting. ___
9 What's that like? ___
10 Where did you say that you went? ___

61

10 REVIEW and PRACTICE

HOME BLOG **PODCASTS** ABOUT CONTACT

Tom and Sam talk about festivals.

LISTENING

1 ▶ 10.5 Listen to the podcast about festivals. Complete the table for the five festivals Anna is going to.

	Country	Type of festival
1	China	_____
2	_____	Comedy and ____
3	_____	_____
4	_____	_____
5	_____	_____

2 ▶ 10.5 Listen again. Write T (true), F (false), or NG (not given) if there is no information in the podcast.

1 Sam is going on vacation with college friends for the first time. ____
2 Anna always goes to festivals in the summer. ____
3 The Shanghai film festival only shows Chinese movies. ____
4 Anna is driving to Edinburgh. ____
5 The Edinburgh Fringe festival is a month long. ____
6 Anna's parents live in New York. ____
7 You can't buy anything at the Santa Fe festival. ____
8 Anna is meeting a friend in Santa Fe. ____
9 Anna is dancing in a competition. ____
10 Anna likes Indian music. ____

READING

1 Read Kate's blog about working out. Match the photos with three of the paragraphs (1–6).

2 Read the blog again. Complete gaps 1–6 with questions a–f.

a I can't move very well in the morning. What is the problem?
b My brother says playing videogames can help us get in shape. Is this true?
c Why do people want to exercise? It's so boring!
d You ran a marathon last year. What did you do when you finished? And are you running any more marathons next year?
e I can't sleep at night and I often get sick. What can I do?
f I went running for the first time yesterday. Why are my knees hurting today?

3 Order the letters to make sports and games.

1 e a t r a k   k_____
2 t a b e l l   b_____
3 w i n s g i m m   s_____
4 s h e s c   c_____
5 c o r k   g l i m c n i b   r_____ c_____
6 g i n s i k   s_____
7 n a s t y g i c s m g_____
8 e k b i   d g i n r i   b_____ r_____
9 l a t e b l a b s k   b_____
10 k i n h g i   h_____

62

REVIEW and PRACTICE 10

HOME **BLOG** PODCASTS ABOUT CONTACT

Our guest blogger and "fitness fanatic" Kate answers your questions about getting in shape and staying in shape.

Questions for a "fitness fanatic"

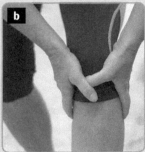

1 _____

I was so hungry after the race. I ate a big plate of rice and a special drink. It's really important to eat a lot after a lot of exercise. But before I ate, I lay down on my back with my legs up in the air – it feels silly but it really helps! As for the future, I'm running the London Marathon next year – wish me luck!

2 _____

I'm sorry to hear that. Were you running on grass or on the sidewalk? Running on hard ground can be really bad for the knees. Try running at the gym. It's less interesting, but it's better for your knees!

3 _____

What type of games is he playing? Because with some games you need to get up and move around. There are dancing games, for example, and games where you pretend you're playing tennis. These games can help you get in shape. But it's much better to actually go dancing or play tennis!

4 _____

I have one word for you – swim! Did you know that swimming every day helps you sleep, makes you happy, and even helps you live longer? And swimmers get sick less than other people. So what are you waiting for? Jump in!

5 _____

Oh, that's too bad! My father had the same problem early in the day. Now he does pilates and yoga every week, and he's like a child again. He jumps out of bed in the morning!

6 _____

There are so many reasons! Some people want to feel good and look good. Other people think exercise is relaxing, and it makes them happy. Do you know the saying "Healthy body, healthy mind"? Exercising can help you think, study, and work. And, of course, it's a great way to meet people!

WRITING PRACTICE

WRITING: Writing informal e-mails

1 Read Sunan's e-mail. Then match sentences a–g with blanks 1–6. There is one extra sentence.

a After that I went to bed.

b Bye for now!

c First, we visited an old castle near Sligo.

d Hi Kristof,

e I hope you're well.

f I wanted to tell you about my vacation in Ireland.

g Then I took the bus to the west of Ireland.

○ ○ ○

To: Kristof Jansson

Subject: Ireland

Attachment: carla.jpg

1 _____

2 _____ How was your summer?

3 _____ I was excited about taking the ferry to Dublin, but the weather was bad, so I traveled to Ireland two days late. So I arrived late, and I didn't have much time in Ireland. But it was beautiful, and it was sunny when I was there.

First I visited Dublin – it's a fantastic city! **4** _____ Carla, a friend, lives in a town called Sligo in that part of the country. She was happy for me to stay with her. But when I arrived at the bus station she wasn't there. She thought my visit was the next week, and she was out of town! I stayed at an expensive hotel that night. Sligo is small, and there wasn't much to do, so I went to a restaurant on my own. **5** _____ How sad! ☹

But the rest of the vacation was great. Carla showed me some beautiful places (see photo).

6 _____ See you next week.

Sunan

2 Complete the phrases with the words in the box.

about   care   hello   how   see   ask   things   well

Starting an e-mail	Asking about the person	Saying why you are writing	Finishing the e-mail
Hi Pete, **1** _____ Greta,	**2** _____ are you? How are **3** _____? I hope you're **4** _____.	Did I tell you **5** _____ ...? I wanted to **6** _____ you ...	**7** _____ you soon, Bye for now, Take **8** _____.

3 Complete the sentences with the correct sequencers, *after that*, *first* or *then*.

1 Juan was late for the exam. _____, there was a problem with the subway. _____ he missed the train. _____, he got lost when he tried to find the college.

2 _____, I found a recipe for chocolate cake on the Internet. _____ I went to the store to buy the things I needed. _____, I made the cake, but I burned it!

3 Helena and Tara wanted to do something special. _____, they went to the park for a picnic, but it rained. _____ they decided to go to the movie theater, but there were no good movies, so they went home.

4 Carlos was tired after a long day at work. He had a coffee and _____ he went to the station, but he fell asleep on the train. _____, he missed his stop and didn't get home until the next day!

4 Write an e-mail to a friend. Tell him or her about a bad or difficult vacation or trip you went on.

- Start and end your e-mail in a friendly way.
- Ask about the person.
- Say why you are writing.
- Use sequencers to show the order of events.

67

WRITING PRACTICE

WRITING: Describing a photo

1 Look at the photo and read Tiffany's e-mail. Then choose the correct answers.

1 What did Ollie do last Saturday and Sunday?
  a He played games.
  b He went to a party.
  c He went to a festival.
2 Where was Tiffany at the same time?
  a in college
  b at a concert
  c in the country
3 What were they celebrating?
  a the middle of summer
  b Rut's birthday
  c the end of exams
4 What did they eat at the party?
  a cold food
  b a barbecue
  c nothing
5 How long was the party?
  a It finished at three o'clock.
  b It finished when it got dark.
  c It continued all night.

To: Oliver
Subject: Hello from Sweden!!!

Hi Ollie,
How are you? How was your weekend? Did you have fun at the festival?

I had a great time last weekend. We had a party at Loke and Rut's house in the country because it was the celebrations for the middle of summer. During the day, we had a barbecue, played games, and swam in the lake. You can see lights at the top of the photo – we put them up because the party lasted all night. But it doesn't really get dark – we took this photo at 3:00 a.m!

Rut is the friend on the right. She's sitting in front of Loke. That's me at the top. I'm standing next to Peter. There are two friends playing guitar. They are Phil and Nikolas – they're excellent musicians! The friend on the left is Trudy, from college. And the friend in the middle, sitting next to Phil, is Nils, Trudy's boyfriend. The other two are Rachel and Danilo, friends of Loke. We had such a good time!
See you soon.
Love, Tiffany

2 Look at the photo and match the two parts of the sentences. Then complete a–g with the correct form of the verb *be*.

1 There __c__   a _____ great night!
2 Loke ____   b _____ a friend from college.
3 Phil and Nikolas ____ c ___is_____ a beautiful red building behind us.
4 Trudy ____   d _____ all listening to music in the photo.
5 There ____   e _____ behind Rut.
6 We ____   f _____ playing guitar.
7 It ____   g _____ two people standing up.

3 Look at the photo. Then complete the text with the words in the box.

| ~~in the front~~ | left | between | right | in the back |

These are people I work with. The woman ¹ _in the front_ with short hair and gray pants is my boss, Maribel. She's fun! The man on the ² _____ with the short black hair is David. He's the receptionist and he's very friendly. Then the older man on the ³ _____ of the photo is Patrick. He's one of the engineers. Another engineer in my office is Gavin – he's behind Patrick. My best friend is Andrea – she is ⁴ _____ of the photo with a book. And that's me on the left, ⁵ _____ Andrea and David. It's a great team!

4 Choose a photo of a party or celebration. Write an e-mail to a friend and describe the photo.

- Explain who the people are in the photo.
- Use the present continuous to say what they are doing.
- Use *there is/are* to say what things are in the photo.

68

NOTES

NOTES

NOTES

NOTES

NOTES

NOTES

Richmond

58 St Aldates
Oxford
OX1 1ST
United Kingdom

Tenth reprint: 2024
ISBN: 978-84-668-2935-9
CP: 880345
© Richmond / Santillana Global S.L. 2018

All rights reserved. No part of this book may be reproduced, stored in a retrieval system or transmitted in any form by any means, electronic, mechanical, photocopying, recording or otherwise, without the prior permission in writing of the Publisher.

Publishing Director: Deborah Tricker
Publisher: Simone Foster
Media Publisher: Sue Ashcroft
Workbook Publisher: Luke Baxte
Content Developer: David Cole-Powney
Editors: Sue Jones, Debra Emmett, Tom Hadland, Fiona Hunt, Laura Miranda, Helen Wendholt
Proofreaders: Pippa Mayfield, Shannon Niell, Jamie Bowman, Amanda Leigh
Design Manager: Lorna Heaslip
Cover Design: This Ain't Rock'n'Roll, London
Design & Layout: Lorna Heaslip, Dave Kuzmicki, emc design Ltd.
Photo Researcher: Magdalena Mayo
Learning Curve **video:** Mannic Media
Audio production: John Marshall Media
App development: The Distance

We would also like to thank the following people for their valuable contribution to writing and developing the material:
Pamela Vittorio (Video Script Writer), Belen Fernandez (App Project Manager), Eleanor Clements (App Content Creator)

We would like to thank all those who have given their kind permission to reproduce material for this book:

Illustrators:
Simon Clare; Guillaume Gennet c/o Lemonade; John Goodwin; Sean Longcroft c/o KJA Artists; The Boy Fitzhammond c/o NB Illustration Ltd.

Photos:
J. Escandell.com; J. Jaime; J. Lucas; S. Enríquez; 123RF; ALAMY/ GerryRousseau, Jim Corwin, Moviestore collection Ltd, Simon Reddy, Stephen French, IanDagnall Computing, Joern Sackermann, dpa picture alliance, Serhii Kucher, ZUMA Press, Inc., All Canada Photos, London Entertainment, Everett Collection Inc, imageBROKER, Pongpun Ampawa, Peter Noyce GBR, Ian Allenden, AF archive, Elizabeth Livermore, Lex Rayton, Ted Foxx, Alvey & Towers Picture Library, Elizabeth Wake, Kristoffer Tripplaar, Lucas Vallecillos, Joe Fairs, Dinodia Photos, Peter D Noyce, Brigette Supernova, Pictorial Press Ltd, Collection Christophel, Jonathan Goldberg, Paul Hastie, Tierfotoagentur, REUTERS, Viktor Fischer, Art of Food, Andrey Armyagov, Alex Ramsay, Blend Images, B Christopher, Judith Collins, David Cabrera Navarro, Roman Tiraspolsky, robertharding, Michael Neelon(misc), Fredrick Kippe, Oleksiy Maksymenko Photography, Patti McConville, D. Callcut, Matthew Taylor, Rafael Angel Irusta Machin, Igor Kovalchuk, MallorcaImages, Paul Quayle, Jozef Polc, Mick Sinclair, Michael Willis, Hugh Threlfall, ITAR-TASS Photo Agency, Bailey-Cooper Photography, jeremy sutton-hibbert, creativep, James Jeffrey Taylor, Oleksiy Maksymenko, Paul Smith, David Levenson, United Archives GmbH, Justin Kase zsixz, Simon Dack, Jeremy Pembrey, Barry Diomede, Alex Linch, Tomas Abad, Valentin Luggen, Sergey Soldatov, Iakov Filimonov, Anton Gvozdikov, Alex Segre, MBI, Paul Gibson, Stocksolutions, MEDIUM FORMAT COLLECTION/Balan Madhavan, allesalltag, David Robertson, Dmytro Zinkevych, Simon Dack News, Vaidas Bucys; CATERS NEWS AGENCY; FOCOLTONE; GETTY IMAGES SALES SPAIN/bjdlzx, Yuri_Arcurs, Reenya, Nikada, Paul Almasy, Martin Rose,

Maskot, Lars Baron, JamieB, Annie Engel, Fosin2, Darumo, BraunS, artisticco, ajr_images, Bison_, AzmanL, artursfoto, pringletta, Dobino, Berezka_Klo, Indeed, Hero Images, KingWu, Tom Merton, NI QIN, Sam Edwards, Portra, ajaykampani, bgblue, leungchopan, c_kawi, s-c-s, kali9, SensorSpot, LeoPatrizi, Talaj, Pix11, Neyya, Dan Dalton, Chimpinski, DKart, shank_ali, Chris Ryan, londoneye, kickstand, kiankhoon, joto, Fuse, skynesher, asbe, gavran333, Zinkevych, KJA, AFP, ViewStock, John Lund/Sam Diephuis, Hiya Images/Corbis/VCG, Tom Dulat, vm, imaginima, TF-Images, Ben Pipe Photography, Ridofranz, PPcavalry, Edda Dupree / EyeEm, Dave Hogan/MTV 2016, Lightcome, Isovector, VikramRaghuvanshi, FaraFaran, Cimmerian, Bet_Noire, David C Tomlinson, Dave & Les Jacobs, unaemlag, technotr, Zoran Kolundzija, tarras79, stockcam, MacLife Magazine, Jetta Productions, Maya Karkalicheva, DGLimages, innovatedcaptures, FatCamera, Power Sport Images, Jasmina81, Lorraine Boogich, Mirrorpix, Kevin C. Cox - FIFA, Purestock, Caiaimage/Tom Merton, Stockbyte, Jason England / EyeEm, Ted Soqui, scyther5, Steven Swinnen / EyeEm, Weedezign, Westend61, Dave and Les Jacobs/Kolostock, chachamal, Cultura RM Exclusive/Frank and Helena, Echo, imagotres, julief514, karandaev, kpalimski, demaerre, Danny Martindale, Art-Y, omda_info, colematt, clubfoto, Allan Tannenbaum, DNY59, stevecoleimages, David Lees, DonNichols, JB Lacroix, asiseeit, Tuutikka, Tarzhanova, Thinkstock, Vladimir Godnik, Uwe Krejci, Venturelli, VladTeodor, Synergee, NurPhoto, Samuel de Roman, nycshooter, RuslanDashinsky, sorincolac, AndreyPopov, AngiePhotos, MistikaS, JGalione, Choreograph, Fotoplanner, Leah Puttkammer, Hero images, John Keeble, Liam Norris, JANIFEST, LWA/Dann Tardif, Ron Galella, Rose_Carson, IvanMiladinovic, Shana Novak, Simon Sarin, T3 Magazine, Floortje, Hung_ Chung_Chih, artlensfoto, domin_domin, Frank van Delft, macrovector, michaeljung, penguenstok, Flashpop, DenisKot, Wavebreakmedia, Creative, Claudiad, Sheikoevgeniya, Philipp Nemenz, Bettmann, Al Freni, EmirMemedovski, wir0man, pshonka, Anthony Harvey, Anadolu Agency, mrak_hr, mixetto, i love images, mbbirdy, kivoart, SnegiriBureau, Rick Friedman, jsnover, iconeer, Monty Rakusen, gilaxia, Maksim Ozerov, gerenme, MStudioImages, MATJAZ SLANIC, andresr, Jupiterimages, Jon Feingersh, adekvat, Jamie Garbutt, Jack Mitchell, Mark Cuthbert, R-O-M-A, Paras Griffin, Peathegee Inc, Radius Images, Gabriel Rossi, FrozenShutter, blueringmedia, davidcreacion, NuStock, justhavealook, reportman1985, zeljkosantrac, Dougal Waters, David Redfern, Askold Romanov, Digital Vision, Krasyuk, Javier Pierini, Marc Romanelli, Neustockimages, Andersen Ross, Alistair Berg, Steven Puetzer, Todor Tsvetkov, Devonyu, franckreporter, Anthony Charles, Danita Delimont, senkoumelnik, ferrantraite, Chesnot, ersinkisacik, bluejayphoto, NicolasMcComber, Photos.com Plus, Robyn Mackenzie, Astarot, Tony Vaccaro, Santiago Felipe, Tristan Fewings, Tetra Images, dogayusufdokdok, nicoletaionescu, praetorianphoto, vgajic, Sofie Delauw, Birgit R / EyeEm, Christopher Polk, PeopleImages, Henn Photography, KavalenkavaVolha, Kittisak_Taramas, tunart, Mike Coppola, Nicolas McComber, Tatjana Kaufmann, LuisPortugal, christopherarndt, Adrian Weinbrecht, Chris Sattlberger, subjug, JuliarStudio, Juice Images, Jrg Mikus / EyeEm, sturti, Roberto Westbrook, Tanya Constantine, Valery Sharifulin, Jason Hawkes, Image Source, IMAGEMORE Co., Ltd., Jacob Wackerhausen, seb_ra, crossroadscreative, m-imagephotography, DEA PICTURE LIBRARY, Hiroyuki Ito, Erik Isakson, EvgeniyaTiplyashina, Hill Street Studios, lushik, Mondadori Portfolio, Andreas Hein / EyeEm, Axelle/ Bauer-Griffin, Emad Aljumah, Deborah Kolb, monkeybusinessimages, Alexandr Sherstobitov, laflor, Michael Ochs Archives, Science Photo Library, BJI / Blue Jean Images, Dan MacMedan, ChrisHepburn, kzenon, Banar Fil Ardhi / EyeEm, PhotoAlto/Sigrid Olsson, Jade Albert Studio, Inc., New York Daily News Archive, Constantinos Kollias / EyeEm, Chris Walter, Photo by Claude-Olivier Marti, Kelly Cheng Travel Photography, Blend Images - Jose Luis Pelaez Inc, shapecharge, Compassionate Eye Foundation/Steven Errico, gbh007; HIGHRES PRESS STOCK/AbleStock. com; I. PREYSLER; ISTOCKPHOTO/ Getty Images Sales Spain, Devasahayam Chandra Dhas, Andreas Herpens, calvindexter, popovaphoto, Phazemedia, denphumi, SolStock, Pali Rao, JoeLena; J. M.ª BARRES; SHUTTERSTOCK/ Glenn Copus/Evening Standard, Olivia Rutherford, MARIUS ALEXANDER, Iakov Filimonov, Sergey Novikov, Blend Images, terekhov igor; Farmer's Daughter; Jono Williams; Andrew Hyde; Aimee Giese; Museum of London; Samsung; SERIDEC PHOTOIMAGENES CD; Telegraph Media Group Limited; ARCHIVO SANTILLANA

Cover Photo: GETTY IMAGES SALES SPAIN/mixetto

We would like to thank the following reviewers for their valuable feedback which has made Personal Best possible. We extend our thanks to the many teachers and students not mentioned here.
Brad Bawtinheimer, Manuel Hidalgo, Paulo Dantas, Diana Bermúdez, Laura Gutiérrez, Hardy Griffin, Angi Conti, Christopher Morabito, Hande Kokce, Jorge Lobato, Leonardo Mercato, Mercilinda Ortiz, Wendy López

The Publisher has made every effort to trace the owner of copyrighted material; however, the Publisher will correct any involuntary omission at the earliest opportunity.

Printed in Brazil by Forma Certa Gráfica Digital
Lote: 800.399